# OUT OF CLUTTER

## FIND SIMPLICITY

Out of Clutter - Find Simplicity
Written by Medha Sarin
Print Edition

First Published in India in 2021
Inkfeathers Publishing
New Delhi 110095

Copyright © Medha Sarin, 2021
Cover Design © Medha Sarin, 2021



ISBN  978-93-90882-41-0



www.inkfeathers.com

# OUT OF CLUTTER

## FIND SIMPLICITY

*Life is simple, yet we make it difficult.*

MEDHA SARIN

Inkfeathers Publishing

*This book is dedicated to my husband Umang Chopra who motivated me throughout the journey of my book and to those souls who want to improve their soul and want to boost their life first. My journey of writing this book was effortless and facile because when it comes to your passion, you find everything easy. I wish after reading this my readers will change their mindset about their perspective of living life and every reader gets their answer about the law of God, about life and human behaviour. So yes this book is dedicated to everyone who has ever been told that 'THEY CAN'T', 'THEIR LIFE IS HELL', 'WORST LIFE THEY CAN EVER HAVE'.*

*Now live your life happily, this was an impetus to write this book.*

# CONTENTS

# INTRODUCTION

Many things people always want to know like about the concept of hell and heaven?

"Why always me?"

"Why god's favourite die first?"

"Why their behaviour is like this?"

I wanted to know all this that's why I am a spiritual coach and psychologist.

This book will tell you the fact which you may search for them till you die.

Some facts never change inside you. These phobias and facts about something. These all aspects have a reason.

Let me tell you my personal experience. My brother is a very good swimmer he used to take me along for swimming, but I have a phobia that I cannot go underwater. He explained to me the technique 100 times he tried his best for years that I learn swimming at least I should learn how to float. I never did because I can't go underwater in a pool or beach we can say I have a phobia. The reason behind my phobia is nothing I never drowned, and I have never seen anyone drowning still I have a phobia. So this book will tell you the reason behind these phobias, behind your unusual behaviour, behind the things you are scared of.

After reading this book trust me you will never judge a soul for his/her phobias, behaviour, and things they get scared of.

Feelings are also the same as you don't decide whether to be an emotional soul, happy soul, or practical soul.

Let me tell you how.

Let's talk about swimming phobia first.

In my last life whether I was a boy, a girl, or maybe some animal  I may drown in the water I may get harmed there. I may have seen something disastrous related to water. My subconscious mind which is our soul has caught this thing. Now let's talk about this life. My life changed, my body changed, and maybe my gender changed but my soul is the same. Let me clear you with one thing that soul is subconscious mind only. We can say soul's mini version. So I came to this life with the same subconscious mind that water is dangerous.  I practised for years my brother did a lot to teach me swimming even a swimming coach did. But still, I don't know how to swim. I love to go to the swimming pool, the beach I love water, but I cannot put my head underwater. Same as feelings if you are an emotional soul since you are a kid. The reason is the same. Souls take millions of years to improve themselves, their phobias, and the things they are scared of. But when we come to this world it takes years but (not a million of course) to improve. It means as a human we can improve our soul faster. Like with a bandage we can heal the wound faster. So here wound is a soul, and a bandage is a human body.

So set yourself free from negative feelings like anger, hatred, jealousy, foolish things. Trust me these things will go with you as your subconscious mind. In Chapter-2 I have explained that how we can set ourselves from any feeling. Like how to control anger, how to avoid the foolishness of people.

If we need our soul to improve. We need to purify that by improving our self in this life.

Do some productive things regularly for your soul, mind, and a good life too. You can improve your life as well as you can prepare your soul for the next one also.

Learn how to find your happiness. Happiness is within us only. While we search for happiness in the world we forget that we only can make ourselves happy.

YOU SHOULD ACCEPT THAT THESE PEOPLE AND SITUATIONS WILL NOT BE MY WAY.

Booklovers none in this world is faultless. We all have some deficiencies, some weaknesses, some culpabilities, some errors. We all have an upright side of us, but then we also have some habituations, some bad traditions that have continued along with us and are rigid to let go of. Have you ever taken note of the spelling of the word HABIT if you take out of it ABIT still remnants now you yield the A out of it BIT still remainders and then if you take out of it still remainders that's undoubtedly why we say OLD HABITS DIE HARD a great Zen teacher named Benzoin had many apprentices? One day the student came up to their teacher Benzoin and reported how they had caught one of their fellow students red-handed as he was stealing something in class, benzoin long-sufferingly heard them out but took no accomplishment. A combination of existences advanced, the same boy was jammed larceny yet once more another stint. And Veen this time the zen master did unequivocally nothing. This infuriated all the students under him who originated up to him and demonstrated that he exercises this boy who was an uncontrollable thief out of his seminary. They further endangered that if no accomplishment was taken against the boy. They will all leave the school. And then Benzoin could have this thief as his only student and teach him in the armistice. The teacher subpoenaed all the students for a meeting when they had all congregated, he said to them, "see you all good boys impending from good people, you all are matured, and you know what is right and what is wrong. If you leave my cool, you'll unquestionably have no trouble in joining some other school. But what about this associate of yours? He indeed is habituated to stealing and I am aware of it. He does not even know the difference between right or wrong. If I reject him, which other school will take him? Who will teach him if I don't? who will put the determination to restructure him, if I don't? I am sorry I cannot ask him to go. It's been wonderful teaching you guys and I would love to have you continue with me. But if because of his staying you want to leave, well who am I to stop you?" Students were stunned by their teacher's answer. Being touched by his empathetic nature and inspired by the values that he held sacred, they decided to stay on. And the boy who had stolen, he had tears rolling down his eyes too. The broad-mindedness and compassion of the Zen master Benzoin transformed his heart. He never stole again in his life later. And his later life became enormously renowned for his integrity. Mistakes happen wrong and sometimes repeatedly. Rather than labelling people as bad, we must reform by sensitivity/ empathy of course, if someone is hardwired to do wrong and does not show any signs of remorse or any signs of improvement and continues to shamelessly abuse the goodness shown to them. Such people may need to be treated differently. But in most cases can transform people with patience and compassion. Remember every saint has a past and every wrongdoer has a future. GIVE OTHERS A CHANCE.

# OUT OF CLUTTER
## FIND SIMPLICITY

# CHAPTER 1

# GOD'S JUSTICE

Well, it will not be possible to understand in few pages or chapters not even books to explain gods' justice your peculiar will proficiency in what accurately 'God Justice' is!!

Many of God's laws have been misinterpreted. Probably the entire world exasperated that up for their survival. Sit in a circle, and have a person start a sentence by susurration it to a person beside him, then pass on the sentence by susurration it to the person beside him then pass on the sentence by susurration it from person to next. Though it reaches the one who started it, it will be unequivocally different. Equivalently, the laws of God Gigantic started from an argument where they were unequivocally precise, but when they conceded down through, the eternities some veracity were reformed. Not exclusively, but comparatively.

Most people think they will do charity; they will help others, no matter what! They will be courteous to everyone, and then they will go to heaven. This is wrong. If we assume that this will take us to paradise and that's why we are doing all these things then we are wrong, totally wrong. Sorry to say but we are being selfish. We need something (paradise) and that's why we are doing all this but not because of our selfless nature. So, we are selfish, not selfless. There is no place in paradise for this thinking. So, make sure that our deeds are selfless. That is what we always go wrong with.

For instance: Most people think that doing charity in many places or to needy people, talking politely, living with a smile, and trying to be a perfect definition of an amazing person with sending you to paradise. We do these things for heaven only not for the improvement of our soul. We think we will do these things then we will go to heaven. We will not go to heaven because we are doing these good deeds for the greed of heaven if we would do these things for the improvement of our soul then the gate of paradise is open to us. Intention matters. Maybe another soul will not get your intention but got will feel your intention. Even doing good things for the greed of heaven will also end up not going there. Only Selfless deeds are pious.

## Many things people always want to know

Is the subconscious mind the same as our conscious mind?

The subconscious mind and the conscious or physical mind are two diverse things. A person can have an extremely advanced intellectual physical mind but may have an underdeveloped subconscious mind. Acquiring worldly knowledge can refine your physical mind but will not develop your subconscious mind. Even psychic knowledge alone will not help your subconscious mind to evolve.

What is the function of the subconscious mind?

The subconscious mind is mutually your shielding light as well as your superintendent light. It presages you when you are about to make a spiritually wrong choice.

For example, when we say 'my heart is denying' this is only your subconscious mind giving you a sign this precise entity is ethically wrong. If we still do that thing we inevitably grieve from culpability and many more things from God Divine

Illustrate: if we have done some unethical deed. After an unethical deed your subconscious mind is not allowing you to forget about it that's GUILT. Imagine you have committed a murder but afterward, you and your subconscious mind spent your whole life recalling it that's guilt is also your subconscious mind is disillusioned with you. But a layer of frightening and not considerate about it is a physical mind who made you do this. There is a layer of physical If every person is having a subconscious mind then who do people follow the wrong path?

At times our physical mind and subconscious mind clashes with our opinion. It's only because our physical mind is coherent occasionally and by the physical mind, people think that this precise thing what they are doing is practical, but the subconscious mind might again it. It is a war between both minds. This is because our subconscious mind opens very little, less than 5%.

Do people frequently ask if hell and heaven even exist? No, as such hell and heaven don't exist. It may depend upon souls. Good souls and bad souls. According to the goodness in their souls is the same as how bad they are. There are 7 realms.

**REALM ONE**

This realm is the lowest and the darkest one and closest to our earth and the most horrible thing anyone can see (I wish none shall experience that). This realm is for the cheapest humans, full of garbage minds and criminal nature. They crawl there under rocks and there is no scope of light in realm 1.

## REALM TWO

This realm is also like realm 1 but little better than that people use terrible languages, hatred, jealousy with each other.

## REALM THREE

This realm is still better but still having no lights and bodies are diminutive lighter as compared to realms 1 and 2. Souls in this realm frequently play blame competitions. And ambition their soul's eminence downwards.

## REALM FOUR

This is much better than in former realms society can see light there and get the chance to improve themselves to go to realm 5, 6 and 7.

In this 21st century, souls are occupied with illicit cognizance, jealousy, detestation, pessimism. 4th realm is also good enough. Apart from the 1, 2, 3 realm at least they can perceive and judge people.

## REALM FIVE

This realm is the foundation of paradise. Here souls are accommodating to each other without any blame games and hatred.

## REALM SIX

This realm is that stunning none can visualize it's just like paradise we say. Souls are upstairs subconscious concentration here. They cannot even contemplate doing what realms 4 and below souls do. As every soul desires to live here but on earth, they overlook a lot, and they commit sins.

## REALM SEVEN

This is the uppermost. This realm is beyond the thoughts. Those are in realm 7 are virtually perfect and purified souls who live in harmony. They help other people to come to a superior realm and even after death they guide souls about their whereabouts.

Even when we are in cavernous sleep, they come to guide us. (We don't reminisce after our sleep what our souls are doing).

USUALLY, SOULS FROM REALM 6 AND 7 DON'T EVEN WANT TO GO TO EARTH BECAUSE THEY KNOW EARTH IS HELL FOR THEM.

If realms are that better then why do souls come to earth?

As compared to the Realm world on earth, souls can progress soon. In the real world, it takes thousands of years to progress but when they go to earth and breathe according to god's law they improve hastily.

For instance: a soul from realm 4 who has gone to earth can come back in realm 5 but can go to realm 1, 2 or 3 also it all depends upon souls' presentation according to god's law.

The reason is in the spirit world we are aware of realms and subconscious mind things so we will try to improve to a higher realm. But in Earth's world, we don't have any awareness of which realm we have come from and where we have to go but still, we will expand ourselves so our improvement will go hastily.

Inferior real souls try to pull higher realms souls down and higher realm souls try to put lower realm to higher realm

Why does God's favourite die first?

Because those souls are from realm 5 or 6. As humans they have gone to earth to progress from 5 or 6 or 7. But regrettable souls from realms 2, 3 or 4 not letting them improve. And God can't see their stunning souls are going to lower realms unintentionally.

For illustrating: Mohan is a pure soul who came from realm 6 want to improve more but his family/ relatives or friends came from realm 3/4/5 they are just pulling Mohan as much as they can it can be intentional or unintentional so God will call Mohan because can't see a pure soul going down.

That's why we say God's favourite is to die first!!

Why do sufferers live long?

Because of their sins, they are sufferers. God gives them a chance to progress themselves

This story with clear you everything:

Mohit is one of the business tycoons. But he is unaccompanied for the reason that he used to beat his wife and she died. He killed his children because he contemplates that they are exasperating and imminent between his work as his wife was dead. He preserved his servants very badly with hunters and all. He was a fraud with his criminal mind, he was an owner of many empires. So, at the age of 70, he met with an accident, and the bones of both legs were dislocated. and now at this age and his bad time none was with him. Normal people like us think he is getting the fruit of his sins. some will say well done, God. But God did this to give him a coincidence; it was not a fruit of his sins. with the ego of his wealth, he did many sins now he has only wealth, not even servants he is all alone taking care of himself. Only God knows without his legs how he is taking care of himself. So now at this time, he reckoned his sins he felt mortified he was cognizant of what he did or what he was doing. He spankings himself often in culpability. In truth, he appreciated his blunders. He called the hospital and demanded one doctor for him as everyone knows him, so they refused. Then he said he will give 50% of his property to that charitable hospital, needy people and he did the same. And another 25% he gave back from where he did fraud and the rest 25% in the guilt of the murder of his kids, he adopted many poor kids and beggars and started captivating care of them. He did all this altruistically for the reason that he realized his mistake. Then he expired fortunately in his 80's. His shoulder came from Realm3 his sins were of realm1 or two, but his shoulder went Realm4.

This is the cause of bad souls who live long and suffer the most. God gives them a chance.

God does everything to expand your soul.

The Subconscious Mind is real you!!

As I have enlightened prior, that subconscious concentration is not but our soul. When we are alive, we cannot see our soul the same as our subconscious mind. We exert according to our physical mind and our own body. But when we die our soul is left with a subconscious mind. Our subconscious mind knows everything, and it provisions everything. But it does not want you to know anything about your aforementioned creation or something because you are here (on earth) for a test, compensating for your karma and working out. So, if your subconscious mind is open you will unquestionably get confused. It only elasticity's gesture when you are exclusively wrong somewhere. So always eavesdrop on your subconscious mind. In other chapters, you will get to know in detail how the subconscious mind works in new ways.

Most Souls have been through lower realms.

For the reason that no soul is here is purest. And pure souls don't even want to come to earth. Anyone is having an envious factor, hatred for someone, bosh minds, criminal minds, or souls with low persistence. Low persistence souls usually contest, shout or hurt others. And if we talk about better souls, they are not essentially the improved they usually pretend to be. For their good image or maybe they think they will go to heaven. Intention matters most of the souls here do good to show off or greed to heaven. At least they are doing good, others are demolished, souls. Some good souls become bad in encouragement and don't want to progress, but some want to progress. God takes them back because in 99 of the bad souls 1 can stay good but can do nothing.

How can we get to know if good souls are guiding us or not?

If our intention is good and we want to improve or we need some solution for that so in our deep sleep (sleep should be without dreams or disturbance) our soul meets another soul who loved us or some good souls from realm6 or 7 who wanted to help us will meet our soul/subconscious mind and guide us. Then we will wake up and our eyes will open with fresh thoughts and new ideas that particular thoughts are the guidance of good souls or souls that love us.

Sleep with dreams means our mind is not at peace.

TIRED BODIES WILL NEVER GET DREAMS that's why people say the empty brain is the devil's house.


## Do not let horoscopes influence you!!

With the horoscopes in newspapers and the internet (weekly horoscopes/ monthly horoscopes)

We read these horoscopes for the reason that we think accordingly we will plan our day, our behaviour, and our situation. This is for brainwashing weak-minded people. everything will happen, it all depends upon you and your karma. If by chance your horoscope is according to you will blindly trust these things if not you will get disappointed. So basically, it is nothing but brainwashing sequences. These days problems are common for every human.

1. Workload

2. Bad Love Life

3. Marriage Issues

4. Family Issues

5. Loss in Business

So, horoscopes have been made so that you can guess your situation. So, if you need a peaceful mind, please stop reading these things. Maybe with this, you destroy your life more.

Unabridged days we see here and there that what's fashionable. So, all is trendy subsequently if the soul is send-off body and take the next body what that soul took along? The earthquake happened in Nepal and many people died. Many people are alive and veterans of that trauma. For those who have seen that trauma there counselling is still going on and about dead ones. They left that body in trauma and took birth as a child anywhere else. What parents understand how their child will be? Faultless. The soul who has seen that discomfort and left-hand that body knows how the kid will be? The kid may fear many belongings, that kid may not go alone anywhere, that kid may not sleep at night alone. That kid may cling to his mother. Now parents are looking at that child and saying, "he is a kid, why is he responsible for this?" because that child's hearing is still pending. Soul has not healed yet. Now that soul can be of a 5-year kid or 50year man they might have seen trauma, betrayal, rejection, and so on. The soul came to a new world with pain. What should that soul take from us? Now, what the kid has seen in his past life if his new parents criticize and say how cowardly you are. We usually do this right? He already has so much pain in his unintentional mind and he is getting criticism here, making fun. So, the influence of that soul will attenuate. Mechanically, this body and age will increase from 5 to 50 but power will diminish in another year because of disapproval and making fun of others, so healer means which will heal every soul.

In the soul, if you are looking at so-called bad things that soul needs more love. Right? So, if I make mistakes, it means my battery is getting low. How low my battery is. I want love, reception, and support. My battery will increase. If I do the opposite, my battery will get reduced. As big as a mistake is, it is the same amount of love we have to give. This is not only for children, but also for everyone who is working around us.

## You can obliterate toxic thoughts directly.

Flowers are in the vessel. When will it start to be conscious in my mind? When I start thinking about it if I don't contemplate it, can it live in my perception? No. how stretched will it live now? Till I will contemplate it. Now that's what reflection gives us supremacy to do. We cannot renovate the world, we cannot change people, we cannot consciously consider our life presence censorious and thoughtful about them because while we are drained that being censorious and perilous about them then it's not about them, it will become a part of our attractiveness. And when I start doing that it's no more about them it's about me weakening my happiness because I am holding on to something in my mind which is not right. So, imagine I don't like that flower I was gossip-mongering about, and I start proprietorship on my mind "awful flowers" they choose the poorest available in the market now when I say the word horrible. The word horrible starts remaining in my mind. Now it's not the flowerpot it's on our cognizance and what is atrocious? It's my acuity about the flower, which is horrible, it's not the veracity of the flower. Because the identical flower is going to be very stunning for you so my observation of the flower, if I create a low vigour word "how horrible" now horrible, is no more outside horrible is the song verified in my mind. And I keep on repelling that song many times a day. What will transpire to my trembling? And then I don't find only one horrible flower. How many people in a complete day don't equal up to our potentials of being factual? If you want to start considering something we can find rather in somebody we are not able to find a solo soul who is 100% seamless. So if I create this pattern of beholding something I will treasure it in each one and I will say he is like this/she is like this (stock all this in mind) do we create thoughts like this? And we feel we are accurate in thinking that way. If I hold a thought about five people, what am I doing to my quivering? And then we assemble back and say they are like this so what am I presume to think about them? And this is where religiousness teaches us that what I think about people very soon becomes a part of my temperament. "Horrible" Is more about them now it's nearby me. "She is so frustrating". Irritating is no more about her, it becomes a part of me. I create a custom of being irritated. Let's do one more homework tomorrow. Tomorrow each one we come across we will look at only one superiority in them. Satisfactory? Now, what will materialize? If we will look up an eminence in everyone it's not going to be about them, where is it all going to be by the end of the day? It will be on my mind. Just underway, placing very high dynamism. She is so sympathetic. I placed the word kind on my mind. He is so modest I placed the word humble on my mind. I have a special idea of what I will become. A little rehearsal? Within a few days where devotion goes will change, not taking care of viewing at paleness is very easy in possession. It is my mind is the coolest. And to hold on for very long comes very much expected of us these days. The same person would have done 100 pleasant things for us what we will not evoke but one that day 10 years back at that nuptial in that corner in that apartment on Wednesday at 9:30 every detail how much we are stuck on its optimal what I indicate to keep in my mind it's my computer it's excellent which records I keep which files I delete. Not occupied maintenance if we are choosing to scratch the stunning files and we are selecting to hold on surplus. And holding on to so much waste we start trusting I am not glad. People are not pleasant to me. The creation is not fine. It's only since of which file, I am observing it on my computer. If someone has said something to me that is not agreeable how much time it will take for me to obliterate it from my mind. How much time? And what to do to eliminate? ABC strolled up to me and thought something undeniably insolent now I prerequisite to obliterate that folder within how many phases to remove? I have to do roughly to erase it if I will not scratch it I will be stuck on it. And if I will not erase it now, I force to stay constantly. what ought I produce to alleged that it would erase instantly? She was impertinent to me in obverse of 1000 people I have to cancel what should I do? What thought do I generate? A thought which instantly swings me for being steady? We have the supremacy how many of you have cured other people's abrasions? Have we restored other people's gashes? Yes. What do we say to them? Fail to recall about it. And I will say how can I disremember that. Now what will you do will you give awake on me...? grasp we adoration people so much we never give up on them. We will keep on motto amusing things to them till when she says ok disremember what she said. Do we do that nope? but we don't assemble back and say these pleasant things to ourselves so what ought I approximately to myself to delete that folder straightaway? What should I say? It's her warmth. Affording to her I am not good. Is it satisfactory for her to have that acuity? Unconditionally adequate. It's her discernment, flora, insolence or maybe it's just her temper just now. But it's all about her. What it has pronounced to me will only imitation her disposition or her current state of awareness to me what am I sensitivity so bad about? I should be curative of her from my affection and dedication for her. Because right now she was in a worrying state of mind to say something which is an upsetting incident, but we get offended, and we exude dual the volume to destructive dynamism. And we are still ranking after 20 years or so. Because still, I am holding it I am glowing it to them on the double extent of the drive. And I am in angled to a person with that adverse vitality interchange because they whispered it to me. I don't say it's they who are distraught, I say they miffed me. Two entirely different comparisons. If I had to just guise at her and say she is dismayed today to declare like this, I would go up to her and rectify her nothing else with my trembling only. But when I say she distressed me I generate 1000 more displeasing thoughts for her. 1 thought can either move me and the other person headed for healing and one thought can shift me towards holding on to that indignant for many years. It is this supremacy to indicate the accuracy in that condition. And when I flinch, consuming that supremacy to produce exact thought in all positions, it's them when I elect to be constant and glad constantly. It's about what I discourse to myself in any position but if I will say "what is this, I am trapped" it's my inward dialogue that will resolve whether I will be joyful, hassled. And who is the originator of the innermost dialogue? We.

Does the state engender my alleged or do I create my alleged reaction to the situation who generates the thought? We. Any situation, who senses someone else producing the thought for you? Can we cancel that 5/10/20 year prevalence right now? How many bibliophiles we can remove right now? What will we have to say to ourselves to erase it right now? We have to say something, it's just not something we will say. Obliterate means I have twisted a thought which sources hurt. I will generate a thought which will reconcile that ache. A thought will miff me, a thought will rebuild me. When I say the truncated regularity thought it originates soreness when I build vigorous right thought I indicate bliss. Cheerfulness In those flashes may not be seamless. But I choose the unspoiled thought exclusively.

Classification is my dominion. It's my empire's upstart. Otherwise, anyone can come outside but no secret. So, to scratch that folder what will I have to do? The previous is very tattered and the other thought is how can I disremember they were so wicked two, unlike things. Third, I don't want to overlook it. Forth one is why should I fail to recall it? There are possibilities. It's only a decision which one I will indicate will decide my vocation. So the previous past it's over. It was their acuity, their disposition, or their temperament that was not respectable that day. Whatever they were maxim or acting it was their character. Lots of love and sanctifications to them. It was unknown to me. The same you will be categorized by diverse different people. Do we even contemplate why? The same me characterized sticky by somebody branded frustrating by nobody else? The same as me. So, who is going to call me fragrant? Why is he calling me sugared? Because he has a very sweet emotion. And if somebody's passion is something else it is because they are comparable to you. assume I am tiring red currently, this is my shade right now, but everybody will see this colour with the lenses they are draining. Somebody will roughly glow and additional will say sapphire. If I attend to everyone, I will overlook my factual shade.

Life was going smoothly. Everything was just fine. And all of sudden, the foundation of life got shaken. Someone who meant everything to us. someone ready to do just about anything for our happiness. Someone who was taking care of us. Their love and respect made our life so fulfilling. Someone around whom our life revolved. Today they are not with us. Their room is empty. We can no longer talk to them. Being in pain and grief, we tend to endlessly blame our fate. That friend talking to whom our cognizance would instantaneously feel relieved Today when we pick up our phone, they are not around to talk to. That colleague who used to be so much fun to work with. Today their chair is empty. Pain is obvious. Grief is obvious…isn't it? What is the purpose or value of life now? And when we look at the country, lakhs of people have left us. What has happened suddenly over the last 2 months? We experience intense pain and sorrow, and we feel extremely angry. We find it natural, don't we? How else can we feel at this time? These feelings are natural, only when we think about ourselves. When we think of what we have lost. What we think of ourselves: All these emotions, feelings, and thoughts. Are very natural. But today we need to think about that soul as well who has left us. But we usually do not think about them. Because we say they have left. It's finished, they are gone. But where have they gone? And what has finished? Their body which was made of the five elements is finished. It was their body that was ill. That body could not be sustained. Their body is finished. But they were not their body. Consider the word 'Human Being' It has two parts, Human and being, human (Jeev) means body. Being (Atma) means the soul. Human means the body which is made of soil. That body is finished about the soul is immortal, it is energy that is eternal and indestructible. The soul who listened to everything we spoke. That soul who could catch our vibration and feelings, despite being distant from us. That soul who could talk to us through their body Even today that soul can listen to our every thought, feeling, and word, and that soul can convey its message to us. Have we thought about that soul who has left? We only spoke about how much we have lost. Of course, we have lost a very important and very beautiful relationship. There is a vacuum created in our life now. That vacuum can never be filled. That is true. But let's think of what that soul has lost. That soul has lost its body. Lost all the relationships. We have lost only one relationship. The rest of our relationship is intact. But that soul has lost all relationships. And also lost all that was possessed and earned over an entire lifetime. The soul does not know where it would go next. On the soul journey. There is a great deal of uncertainty within about how the future will be… which family they will be going into, next… That soul who has moved on has lost everything. So, who is in greater pain? We have lost one relationship: That soul who has moved on has left behind the body and all relationships. Besides losing everything earned and possessed during this lifetime. They don't know where they will be going next. They do not know what will happen to them there. Whose pain is more and whose insecurity is more?

As you have moved on to play a new part Whose pain is more and whose in insecurity is more whose square is more we need to think we were so deeply coached up inner on the pain that we hardly thought about them subsequently all pain and all a kept reaching them as ambiances today let's all get together we shall be organized understand these little things and what and how to think at this time? About what and how to think at this time and how to create thoughts that will sanction them? Thoughts that will elasticity them dialogue that will give them sanctifications this is very imperative when a soul leaves the body after leaving the body that's all new interchanges forward on its expedition where is that solve come from that's all has cross the threshold the worm of its new mother we need to appreciate this and we need to start farsighted it visualise this scene that's all has entered the bomb of its next mother but the new physique which is accomplishment ready there in the home and the new intimate where the in the black red present that's all has no construction accessory with the new family this all does not unfluctuating know them that's all is a assessment only with us with our family with this family when the soul has left overdue so bring this seen on the screen of your mind that's all is in the form of a mother it is able to catch our every alleged it is able to eavesdrop to every word every feeling that we involvement is accomplishment that's all that's all which has moved forward after losing everything should we be sending to that's all in grief and what is? When that's all was with us, we were willing to do the whole thing for the cheerfulness even nowadays we need to be ready to do anything for them vitamins before therapeutic your discomfort let's see that's all let's make their mind authoritative first the new intention is approximate to instigate a new body is being paid fashioned at this time, we ought to be municipal of that explain be?? Will connectivity do that for everyone we will definitely do that for all the shows we know but there are millions of souls we have moved forward on a new journey we do not even know them but they are also in need of cosiness supremacy and harmony at present for the reason that they left their body when many other left as well and when numerous solve leave instantaneously email Spain is created the state in which they left and the farewell they received there was a lot of blankness and the evolution itself was half-finished so we all have a responsibility we cannot fall to simplify get angry and when we read or was about souls departure the body will certainly feel bad but we also prerequisite to reminisce our accountability communally we have a obligation of construction them authoritative with the blessings and supremacy so that going forward they will have a beautiful elevator destiny come let's bring them on the screen of your mind for a few moments take a look at yourself in the centre of your forehead at tiny point of light .I am a soul. I am the energy who drives the body I am a soul this body is a costume which I have won it is my costume now visualise that personality in anterior of you they are also our soul a argument of light energy there were Divas their clothing it was a uniform they are an interior Imperishable solve my affiliation is not with their uniform or clothing mix a ship is not with their physique in my listen send is with them it is the atmosphere to Soul construction it was an affectionate association it is the existing affiliation and will continuously be that way I the atmosphere I will yield care of you previously considerate for myself your state your peacetime of mind and your solidity they are my chief errands from me you shall accept trembling of transparency amity and influence purity peace and power full trembling are reaching you are protective shield of Gods powers is always with you are endangered when someone shrubberies us unpredictably and move advancing on the soul excursion are mind turn out to be very squirmy and obstacle grouchy with anticipate about them and yell we also almost how could you endorsement us like this and go did you not think about us? Think about how we will accomplish without you? So many more accountability to shoulder together and you left us Equidistant the Mind promotions a lot of interrogations and grievances there is anguish but that anguish becomes a grievance by grumbles let's appraise the sports for an instant and intentionally transformation our thoughts let's remember that our every thought is reaching that's all remind yourself repeatedly my everyone thought my every feeling my every word my every vibration is itching that soul who has left the body having these them it is affecting their state of mind and the new body which is getting formed in the form of the new mother is every thought is affecting the health of that body which is formed so what vibration do we want to send to that's all? Homes and spending a lot of time with the stores gave us a lot of joy and took care of us and it's so much for us but then there came a time when they had to leave and go elsewhere when they are set to leave what do we say to them? Influence them to stay back for some more time we say please take back it is such a preference to have you here but they say I too feel like staying back but I have some exertion to take care so I need to go there which means we don't feel like sending them off but how do we meet them when they authorization? We approximately bye acknowledge you so much for actuality with us we had an attractive time with you we see them off with the lot of gratitude for their occurrence and time we don't feel like sending them but with acknowledge them before their take leave for the reason that those few are spent in their corporation were tremendously attractive and unforgettable therefore while keen-sighted them off we proposition our genuine thanks we do not criticize but this all who are departure us now throughout this epidemic they are going to a place from where they cannot reappearance but they left too soon it they had stayed on more few more years we could have done so much organized that is the 10 the number of years they could have been with us and we could have been with them instead of thinking this way let's give gratitude that we will together for all these years do not send them the energy of complaints send them an energy of gratitude for every Breath gratitude for every single thing they did for us gratitude for their perfect personality which was filled with beautiful Sanskar they there are so many things to be grateful for so our memories should not be filled with complaint Sanga or emptiness let's be full of gratitude for the time spent together and when we complain that they left us suddenly remember that it's only the body that is finished this all is not amongst us anymore but their thoughts and feelings even now the vibration of their thoughts reach US it is not that they have left us alone and moved on even now they will advise you and guide you even now if you need any important decision just think of that solve and ask you will experience that the soul is indeed giving you and answer so even after going away from us they have not left us they continue to be with us through the state of mind for example when someone goes abroad they are physically away but we are connected to them in our minds we even catch their feelings so from today we will not remember With complaints, our complaints do not have any energy. Let's bid them farewell with gratitude. Will they feel comfortable if they receive complaints from the US? They are always so helpless as they cannot come back at least let us and them vibrations which will horizontal soothe them they should feel good about every moment that they spent with us let's finalize today that we will only keep giving gratitude we will always give them only gratitude to that soul and also gratitude to God because we had the fortune of such a beautiful relationship with a beautiful soul that's all spent so many years with us they made our lives of Wolf King thank you to God and thank you to that's all bring that's all on the screen of your mind and look at them and today we will gratitude to for every incident and every memory greater together I am loving soul life is my Sanskar I the soul respect everyone I need Nothing from everyone why this all m a giver I am a selfless all you gave me a lot of love for all these years every moment spent with you was filled with love and respect I received so much from you I cannot thank you enough thank you very much thank you for your beautiful nature for all your Sanskar I am grateful thank you for your behaviour for all your elevated karmas I am grateful. Your every relationship, your every responsibility, you manage them all perfectly. How much for all your services? As you have moved on to play Anup path to play a beautiful role and hence you have moved forward. The love and blessing of God who is the ocean of love are always with you. The love and benediction of God is the ocean of love and is always with you. Gratitude to you. Gratitude to God. Thank you. Many of US are experiencing a sense of guilt or helplessness are mind is repeatedly saying if only we had admitted them in that hospital if only we had done so and so if we had called up that other place for oxygen if we could not do anything for them the mind becomes very restless as we hold ourselves responsible the person we reached out to could not help us never mind but why did I hesitate to call someone else is mind repeatedly keeps questioning this wale and the Mint pili blame us and for our family member leaves the body besides some of us have also received a phone call from people, request. Play wanted to help. We're not able to help. pad not available, oxygen was not available. Head ka best. Peer holding as responsible. With such thoughts, we feel extremely helpless. Many of us feel when they were in the ICU and especially in the final days, we were not with them. At the hospital and left with no one and thoughts bring a feeling of anger towards ourselves. That someone needed us in their family moments, but we were never there for them will let them remain alone in the hospital. Some say if only we had fought with the doctors and got into the ICU at least for a few minutes. We would have at least met them once. There is no such thing created. This guilt does not trouble only the US this also affects the Destiny of the soul who left us. 1 minute evaluate the kind of vibrations they are receiving from the US. We could not do certain things for you, we could not save you. Who as much as we should have done? We think and say to ourselves I did not try harder. I should have done much more. I am not good at Karma. I did not do good Karma. All these vibrations reached that's all and we were not with you. Can reach that resolution now let's focus on the other side. A new mother and a new body is getting from there a child's gravity getting created in that womb. But by vibration is that body or that's all getting there? Do anything for you. We are not good. We did not take care of you. We left you all alone. We were not with you when you needed us. All these repeated thoughts which we create are credited to the soul who is in the womb. garb Sanskar means the vibrations which are solved while in the womb the thoughts and feelings which that all catch this and scars of this all are created based on these vibrations. What is the vibration that's all Catching? Not with me when I need it. My family did not make any effort to help me. My family did not take care of me. That's all it takes to catch such a vibration. Think and everything we speak that's all will catch it and believe it to be the truth. Because they are constantly catching your vibration. Getting vibration while in the worm it gets very strongly recorded on this all. Hindu child will be born into a new family that might be very loving and takes very good care of that child. When will it revolve around the child throughout the day? But that's all recorded by vibration while in the warm. Take care shop me. Not love me. Army. They're not with me when I need them. The messages which had been sent. That child no. That's all it takes to wear the dress of a child. The Destiny of the child. 12834 for 5 years old even if the family is caring very well but The Sanskar and the dip recording in that child will be no one to take care of me. no. day. no. Then. Trying to explain to the child. wear where? Does our entire day revolve around you? Revolves around you? The child will insist that you are not there for me when I need you. You people leave me alone. Life becomes a struggle for the child there. Experience a lot of pain. They will feel lonely and that no one is with them. Even though they have a caring common family, why did Sanskar get created in that child? Why did the child record these thoughts and feelings while in the worm? Garbh Sanskar soft bi child? We created such thoughts for the school. Short? Direction to this all? The problems and struggles in their life? Play whatever thoughts we created were true? They are not true. We made a lot of effort to save them. We went everywhere and we tried everything we could. Then why do we say such things especially when they are not true? We were not let into the ICU because it is the rule. Everyone was safe but in our minds, we were always connected with them. Even today we are thinking of them then why are we creating wrong thoughts and words about our efforts? And word is forming the basis of a new destiny and new life for that problem. For their relationship with the new family. Is vibration based on their Sanskar? Let's think carefully and think right. From today let's change your thoughts and send them a message as we know no, we did everything for you. We didn't do things which we earlier had no idea how to do, we went to places where we had never been before. We did everything many times more than our capacity. They put everything, body, mind, and wealth to save you when you were in the hospital. We were not with you physically but mentally we were only and only with you. Even today we are only and only with you. Right thinking. We need to use this vibration to create their Garbh Sanskar. The operation will influence the body that is getting created in the worm they will influence the relationship of that solution. Create an elevated Fortune for that problem. Possibility. The queen of your mind for a few moments. You were sending them Bentley. And send them messages which are through. Tell them about how much effort you put in not because you want to prove anything to them. But do it only e so that Pradeep truth accurately that they had a very loving family which was ready to do everything for them. That their family was always available we need to record this Garbh Sanskar for them. I am a pure soul. My every thought is pure. My every word is filled with respect. Being selfless I take care of everyone. I serve everyone. I always took care of you. I always obeyed you. Whatever was right for you I did only that. We gave our everything and served you with our body, mind, and wealth. Sometimes, physics with you. But mentally we were always with you. We are with you even today. Continued to be with you. Mai is always with you. The ocean of peace God's vibrations of peace is feeling you completely. You are peaceful. You are powerful. We never imagined that our loved ones would leave us all of a sudden. Had just developed a slight fever, coma, and light breathing difficulty. We were getting them good treatment at home. to get them admitted to the hospital. But we were certain that they would come back so we did not discuss anything else with them. We are focusing only and only on their treatment. All of a sudden accommodate ab on their journey, leaving us behind. There was so much that was left unfinished.

We had so much to say to them. We had so many things to ask them. We wanted to ask how to manage everything, but we needed to do it. Then we share our feelings as well. Fund. Questions like I want to know and what they wanted to tell us. Add so much to convey. Only when the body is finished, continue to listen to everything and think. Two can catch every message that SOL is creating a forest. Provided movies are ready for it so first of all we will change one thought. I could not convey my message to them. Ask all the questions that were on my mind. This week we can never get our mind or our message across to that soul. When someone leaves with us but when they travel to another city or even go to or go to our school office sometimes, they travel to another country. Sometimes we even send Sitcom events if things are not going right with them there. Call them up and ask if everything is fine. They tell me everything is fine. What happened? and then how did we know when they were worried or unwell there? How could we sense that something went wrong at their school? How did we sense it all? Allopathy means our thoughts reach them and their thoughts reach the US. It happens with us and with everyone else too but when the soul leaves the body e when it is out of the body all of us have heard about an out-of-body experience. Also, I can hear everything and understand everything during an out-of-body experience. At present, the soul has left the body. It has entered a new body but this call is not yet connected or attached to the new body. Show the soul which has left the body in our family. Its state is also the same. As when they were with us in their body. They were able to catch our messages and we were able to catch them. Of course, we could do it only sometimes, and additives. But right now, since they are that's, all are detached from the body. That's all 100% at the moment. Are catching our every thought and vibration. The message they want to send us is also very powerful. So, please share whatever is on your mind right now. It could be something from the past, it could be about forgiveness it could be something from the past, it could be about forgiveness it could be gratitude even if you wanted to share something with that's all you can do all that now have complete faith that you are not just saying something casually, but they are catching your messages. When someone is with us, sometimes we explain things but still, they cannot understand. And we get upset that they are not able to understand us. Sometimes it even creates some misunderstanding. But when your soul leaves the body, its power becomes very pure and clear. Not just catch your words, that's all will also Catch your intention and feeling. Social everything that is on your mind. Anything. If there are any Nani mistakes or any conflicts, if we feel we have not asked for forgiveness we can do it right now. Aur, if we had not given them something, we can do it right now. We tend to say their mistake was negligible. I wish they would come back and now that I have given them time? Right now, it feels negligible but when the incident happened that mistake was and that incident was already recorded on that soul. That they had made a mistake or that they were not right to you. You can forgive the problem now. Your vibrations of forgiveness will influence their new destiny and a new body.

Your right sensations are very imperative for their state of mind and their Sanskars at present. So, say whatever you want and ask whatever you want. Thank them. Exonerate them and even ask for understanding. If you had not shared approximately what they were supposed to know, tell them today. If there is anything on your mind, inform them and drop the burden. Tell them the whole thing and ask them what you want. It is not that only our vibrations are reaching that soul. Their vibrations are reaching us too. But to catch their message, we need to keep our minds peaceful and stable. The more we think right, the more we think only the truth. The more we keep our minds peaceful and stable. And when we reminisce about that soul with love and gratitude. Not with pain or complaints. Then our catching power will increase. When there is a lot of disturbance here, we cannot catch their vibrations. It is like, we cannot talk to someone when their phone is engaged. So, silence the noise here. Then you can receive the message they are conveying. And you will understand it as if they are standing right in front of you and explaining. Intuition which we experienced with them even earlier. although it was happening only at times. Now we can experience it continuously. We must keep our minds peaceful and stable. say everything you want to, and ask the whole thing you want to. We will do it right now. You can rehearse it every day. That relationship continues even at present, it is not a matter of the past. It is a soul-to-soul connection. Never say I "had" an affiliation. You still have that affiliation and will always continue to have. Come, let's share everything that is on our minds with that soul.

I am a powerful soul. The almighty authority, God, is always with me. I am protected. I, the soul, share everything that is on my mind with God. My mistakes, my weaknesses, I surrender everything to God. From God, who is the ocean of knowledge I receive the right understanding. I have an understanding of the right thoughts and the right karmas. I get solutions for all my problems from God's teachings. Now, bring that soul on the screen of your mind. Whatever you have on your mind, any incident from the past, if you need to seek forgiveness for anything from them or if you need to forgive them for anything if there is something you want to tell them or if there is something you want to ask them to share everything with that soul.

Many of us have a pang of deep guilt. We say- "I was the first one to be infected by Covid at home." "And because of me, they got infected." "I recovered, but they left the body..." I am the reason for their death. I am the cause for the grief of my whole family. Because of me, everyone's life in our family has changed. We are repeatedly telling ourselves- "I am the cause." We are blaming and cursing ourselves, believing we no longer have any right to live. Since we think the unfortunate events happened only because of us. If these vibrations reach that soul who has left, is it good for them? Moreover, is it the truth? Is this vibration good for the soul whose 'Garbh Sanskar' is getting created? Is it good for them to create a soul recording or this time? That- someone close to me, someone from my own family", my own family or friend was responsible. Because of that, I lost everything. Do you want to record this message on that soul who has moved on? Do we understand what happens if it gets recorded this way? They will not be able to trust any family member or friend in their new journey. They will always carry an unknown fear. A fear that "any of these people can be a cause of my misery, any of them can harm me." I might lose everything because of them. That soul will start feeling this way in the new life. Because it got recorded while they were in the womb. As "I lost everything because someone was very close to me." Why did it get recorded? Because we have been saying it. Someone we even tell each other. Sometimes we even create thoughts for that soul as "It all happened because of you. Should you not have taken care?" You went out and caught the infection, and now look at what happened to my life. All these things might seem true. But it is not the complete truth. The destiny of every soul is created based on its Sanskars and karmas. When a soul takes a new body, which means when a child is born, the child carries a destiny into that birth. That is why many parents get horoscopes prepared, soon after a child is born. How is that child's destiny determined on the day- one of birth? Because the Sanskars and karmas carried by the child determine the destiny of that child. The timelines of a majority of huge situations that would occur in the child's destiny are written in that horoscope. Of course, some of those things will change eventually, but some of them remain accurate. Some of those things will change because a child will change certain Sanskars, along the journey. Therefore, some aspects of their destiny will change. But today, we need to finalize one thing, this needs to be internalized once and for all. That is the soul who spent a beautiful time with us all these years. It was time for them to move forward into the next role. It was time for them to leave. We always question why they left. They have a new role waiting and that was a reason to move forward. That soul has a special role to play now. There is so much happening, as this world is transforming. This world needs to transform, and that soul has a special role in it. That is the reason the soul has moved on. The soul has not gone because of me. The soul leaving us was already decided in their role, in their destiny. The course or reason for moving on could be anything. Why were they destined to leave? Because we were destined to be together only for a specific duration. And thereafter, they had to move on to play a very special role. That soul had to play a different part and do something special for our country or our world. We don't know where they went or why they went. But it was important for them to move on. They are supposed to do something else according to their destiny and hence they have left. Therefore, do not hold yourself responsible. Holding yourself responsible will not only give pain to you and your family. But it causes maximum pain to that soul who has left. Because they will record only whatever they hear from us. We need to take care because everything which we think and speak will reach them and get recorded on that soul. Our vibrations will radiate to them and get recorded on that soul. We need to think and speak carefully. While thinking and speaking we need to visualize that everything is getting recorded on them. Do we want them to record that their family member or friend was the cause for everything?

Moreover, it is not the truth. Our karmic accounts and our destiny these two entities are with us at every moment. No one else can either create our destiny or ruin it. We hold the pen to write our destiny. And we create our destiny, based on our elevated karmas and Sanskars. And when someone leaves us, it doesn't mean their destiny was bad. It doesn't mean that they had done wrong karma, or we had done wrong karma. Not. Our fortune is not determined by the number of years we were together. It is decided by the quality of our relationship. By the quality of our Sanskars and Karmas. That soul was supposed to move on, for some other elevated purpose. To play a new part, it was already decided in the destiny. About the duration for which the soul would be with us and thereafter move to a different place. So, take a few moments to convey this message to the soul. It is very important to send the right message. Do not create incorrect recordings on the soul. And do not allow incorrect recordings to get imprinted on that soul.

I am a wise soul. The incorporeal supreme soul, God who is the ocean of knowledge has explained to me all the facets and secrets of knowledge. I am a wise soul. God's love and God's blessings are my strength, my powers. Truths about the soul, knowledge of the karmas, awareness of the cycle of birth and death- I have understood all of them. In this drama of life, every soul is playing its part. Everyone's role is fixed. After completing their present role every soul moves forward to play their next role. It is the part that belongs to that soul. I cannot change their part. Their parts are very lovable. Their part is fixed. Now, visualize that soul in front of you. And say- "please forgive me." "Please forgive me for some of the karmas that I did unknowingly." You played an extremely beautiful part while you were with us. You have now moved forward, to play another elevated part. I, the soul, have understood this well. I, the soul, accept the truth. I accept it completely.

Whenever we head out of home for a few hours. We might be going out for work. Children and other family members might be at home. At such times we will have just one intention of setting everything at home before we leave. So that, in our absence there shouldn't be any problem at home. We have such a pure intention for our family that everything should be set and smooth. Sometimes when we need to travel for a few weeks or months, to a different city or country. While we are there, we call up our family. We enquire about everyone's well-being. What do they say? They tell us- "all of us are doing well. You don't worry." Then we ask them specific details- "what about that work was supposed to be done. How are you managing it?" They will again insist- "do not worry about us. We are fine and that work is going on fine." You just focus on settling down well there. This was our intention, isn't it? Whether we were away from home for a few hours, days, or months. Today, look at yourself. If we leave a family behind forever, which if we leave the body and move on. What do we want to hear from our family? What do we want for them? Won't we have just one intention- that everything is set and smooth for them, even after we leave? That no one is put into any kind of inconvenience? Will our mind not feel relaxed by just listening to that? That is our responsibility today. If we keep repeatedly thinking and speaking about someone who has left the body as- "how will we live without them? How can this house function without them?" There is no more purpose to my life. I should not have been alive. I too should have gone with them. Who will take care of children now? Who will take care of me in my old age? If we keep thinking and speaking this way. what vibrations with that soul who has moved on, get from us? That soul is now in the womb of a new mother. And is catching our every thought, word, and vibration. Do we want to send such painful energy? That soul cannot even come back. But if we keep sending such vibrations, will that soul be able to settle down this?

We are trying to pull them back so that they should somehow return. Is that right when we send a message- "this house cannot function without you?" Is this energy right for that soul? For one moment, visualize you're in their position. You can neither come back nor can you settle down there. And you repeatedly receive painful thoughts from your previous family. How will your state become? That soul had been through so much, before moving on. Their bodies had become extremely ill. Don't we all want their new body to be very healthy? Don't we all want that their mind should be peaceful and fearless now? So, what vibration should we send to that soul? From today, let's practice this and it is very simple. We will do it every morning and every night. We can also do it any number of times during the day, whenever we remember this aspect. But we will certainly do it every morning and every night. So, every morning and night, we will specifically think of them. We will give them god's powers and blessings and convey one message to them every day- "we are absolutely fine here." "Please do not worry about us." "We are all here together, with each other." "We are taking very good care of each other." "We will continue taking care of everyone." "You have given us so much and taught us how to care." "On that basis, we will take care of all the family members." "You please do not worry about any of us." "Be completely free from any sort of worry about us." "You just take care of yourself there." "Do not have any concerns about us. We are fine." When these thoughts reach that soul there because all that soul wants is to listen to just this one thing. The soul wants to catch just this one message that the previous family is doing fine. The soul needs to know this. Therefore, we need to clearly say it and we cannot afford to say the opposite of it. Because all those painful thoughts which we feel are right, actually are not right. They are not right for us; they are not right for the rest of our family members. And most importantly, such thoughts are not right for the soul who has moved on. Because that soul just wants one thing- "my family (who I have left behind) should be fine." "My job or business should be running smoothly." "For all the effort I had put in, everything is going fine." So, whether it is children, parents, spouses, or siblings of that soul. All of them need to create these thoughts for the soul who has left. Repeat these thoughts every morning and every night. Fill your house with purity and positivity. Play songs of god's remembrance in the house, throughout the day. Play songs that have high-vibration words, so that everyone's minds become peaceful and powerful. A then the vibration of your peace and power will reach that soul as well. Bring back your life to normal as soon as you can. The vacuum that is created can never be filled. It will continue to remain. But that relationship will continue. We will not feel a lack of relationship, because we continue to exchange vibrations with that soul. But the sooner we bring ourselves, our family, and our house towards normalcy. The better that soul will feel in their new journey. They will get the feeling and assurance that everything is fine at home and in business. For that soul to feel that way to catch and get the right message from us. It is important for their journey. Do not try to pull them back through your thoughts. Do not keep asking them to return. That soul will feel stuck, as they can either come back or settle down in their new journey. let's not think only about ourselves. Even earlier we had been selfless. We were always thinking about their well-being, and they were thinking about ours. We need to continue doing it even today. Let's create these right thoughts every morning, every night, and any number of times throughout the day. Just say those lines while working or if there is any problem or if you don't understand something. Immediately Create a thought for that soul- "don't worry, we will learn and we will do it." "Even otherwise, we will find out from someone else." Our message is reaching that soul. And bring back your home towards normal activity, at the earliest. If everyone returns to eating well, sleeping well, and taking care of themselves. That is exactly what the soul who has moved on, wants from you. That all of you are taking care and doing fine. Come, let us send them this very important message. We will first internalize it well, and send it to them with all our hearts. That soul will then be able to accept our message and become worry-free.

I am a happy soul. God, who is the ocean of happiness, absolves all my sorrow. He fills me with the power of happiness. In every situation, my mind remains stable. My mind remains peaceful. Everyone receives comfort and happiness from me. God's hand of blessings and companionship are always with me. I, the soul in every scene of life, experience God's help. As I take one step of courage. God's multi-million steps of help are always with me. Now visualize that soul in front of you. Say to them- "do not worry about us." "All of us are fine here." "We are taking very good care of ourselves and each other." "You have taught us everything that we needed to know." "Thank you very much." "Your teachings, as well as God's powers are always with us." God's powers are always with us. Always with us.

Every year, we celebrated their birthday. We flooded that soul with blessings. "Happy Birthday, have a beautiful life." "Have a healthy body." We would fill their life with blessings. We would certainly do this on their birthday every year. And also, on many other special occasions. We would bless that soul every day. Because we bless our family daily. But at present, are we blessing the soul who has left us? This is the time when their new journey is about to begin. A new body is getting created for that soul. A new relationship is getting created. A new Destiny is getting created. A new life is about to begin, for that soul. Are we giving good wishes and blessings to that soul? Have we told them- "happy new life... healthy new body..." "Beautiful new relationships...? amazing and powerful new Destiny." Have we blessed that soul for a new life? Have we blessed them as "your new body will always remain healthy?" "Your new relationship will be very beautiful." Your new fortune will be extremely elevated. Have we said all this to that soul? Is it not important to tell them? When we were saying it every year on their birthday, on other special occasions. This is a time when their new life is about to begin. So it is all the more important to bless the soul right now. Because our blessings and good wishes will have a huge impact in making their new Destiny, extremely elevated. From today let's not create vibrations of complaints, pain, or grief. We shall think of them with love. We shall think of them with gratitude. Our thoughts should comfort them and make them worry-free. And most importantly, we shall think of them and send blessings. Come, let's send all these good wishes and blessings beside any other blessings you wish to give them. Send blessings to everyone. We shall collectively send blessings and good wishes to everyone, and specifically to that soul.

I am a loving soul. In the soul, radiate Love to everyone. I, the soul, am nurtured by God's blessings. God's blessings make my life easy and simple. In the soul, give blessings to everyone. Now visualize. not just that one soul, but visualize all the souls in front of you. And bless everyone- "you are a pure soul." "Your mind is filled with happiness." "Your new body is perfectly healthy." "Your new journey is a very happy one." "Your new family is extremely loving and happy." "You have moved forward, to play a beautiful part in the task of world transformation." "All of us offer to all of you, our gratitude." "Thank you. thank you very much." "And plenty of blessings to all of you." "Blessings... blessings to you." We all light candles. Come, let's light a Divas of blessings today.

# CHAPTER 2

# SET YOURSELF FREE FROM FEELINGS

It simply means if you are a good soul feeling betrayed, hurt, anger, and spoil your soul only.

So just set yourself free from any feelings and it's not possible that every time you may be right.

For assistance, you are a wife who made paneer for your husband. He ate it and said this paneer is amazing but not as my mother cooks it. After saying this he leaves for office. Now while appraising this, you will think, "I will get hurt while eavesdropping on this." "I made paneer and my husband compared my paneer with his mother's", you will think about this for the whole day. You made much in your mind while thinking about many things related to this. You may call your mother/ friend and talk about this and in return, you want to listen-"Oh no, he said this very wrong" and if they say the same you will get more hurt maybe you will start crying. you can even think "he may not love me".

So, you spoiled your day with all this. Then your husband came back. He was not at all aware of what's happening in your mind for the whole day and he was cold-hearted and asking you about your day and you lashed out because you mushed your mind.

So, if we discuss this example in a very unpretentious way, according to your husband's statistics, her mother makes paneer better than you may be, according to your brother, the statistics can be approximately diverse. The fact was not according to you that's why you mushed your brain. Diverse minds have diverse facts.

Equivalent as you wore a dress in pink your husband applauded you and the same dress in yellow, he didn't so according to him the fact that he likes you in pink maybe some of your friend's commendations for you in yellow.

We people don't understand the facts of the other person and we overthink like anything.

Like this only we waste our whole day in tiny things and forget to live life peacefully.

The situation cannot always be according to us.

In the same paneer's example, if there is no matter of fact instead of fact, he is impertinent to you and still, you should calm your mind. In the previous chapter we learned that if someone is doing bad, he will someday feel remorseful. With this, you are also progressive your peace, time, and coddling your health.

In these two cases, you were right no matter what it was fact or insult. So proudly smile and move on. Don't make all this wrong at your end with crying, hatred, or some other feeling.

With this, you will always live a guilt-free life, and trust me it is the best life anyone can ever live.

No hard feelings will only make you stronger with a beautiful smile.

Insulting someone will also make you or your soul/ subconscious mind guilty.

We cannot fool our subconscious mind...!! trust me.... never!!

## YOUR SMILE CAN CHANGE YOUR LIFE

Yes, your smile can change your life. It means it's all about positivity.

1. Positivity for living life

2. Positivity for handling hurdles in your life

3. Positivity in wickedest conditions

Your vibration for any situation is more important than your reaction. Because reactions come from the physical mind and body and vibes come from the subconscious mind and soul.

So, if we talk about positivity for living life. Anyhow, we have to live a life now it depends on us how we will extravagance ourselves in this life. It's all depends on how we respond to a circumstance.

For assistance: Mohan is preparing for a competitive exam. He has given his day and night for that exam. He has given 3 attempts. He is not getting any optimistic results, still, with a smile, he tried for the 4th attempt. It all depends on how you will take that failure. He didn't consider that failure as a failure he considered that failure as an experience and practiced more and more with a good vibration he became more focused. instead of thinking why he has not cleared, he was trying to find out where he is lacking. So finally, he cleared in the 4th attempt.

Only a few people do this theory 'try again and again' else people will posterior ready, or they may attempt suicide in hindrance.

Nothing is more important than positivity for living a good life.

With negativity, you can attain nothing. A negative mind can destroy your whole life.

A negative mind can make you suffer. But you will never suffer in a positive mind as you read the story of Mohan, he could be a sufferer. But he thinks only a positive mind can give you a good life.

Numerous hurdles will come in your life between your living, but God will help those you help themselves.

Never do wrong, stay positive and guilt-free. Smiles will inescapably come to your beautiful face.

One more assistance.

Mohan disrespected Rohan purposefully and Rohan said nothing, not even a word. So, the guilt of an insult will be inexorably on Mohan maybe not on his physical mind but his subconscious mind. Rohan didn't impute his soul. Rohan's thoughts should be "maybe Mohan is not well", "maybe he doesn't like me", "maybe he is trying to show himself" in any way Rohan is not wrong.

So, this is one situation that Rohan can handle.

Now the second situation can be "Mohan disrespected me", "he is desirous of me", "now see what I will do", "I will insult him more" this status quo is not at all optimistic. With Mohan Rohan's soul also will be with culpability.

Now if we talk about the POSITIVITY OF HANDLING HURDLES IN LIFE so hurdles are like speedboats on road for vehicles. It can come anytime but if we will cross our obstacles we can go slickly if we don't adjoin ourselves to negativity.

Hurdles are like a test. If this test does not come, we will forget to study. If hurdles do not come, we will forget to value the importance of happiness in life.

For assistance: Mohan has a perfect life = A good job without hard work, A perfect relationship, Healthy life, and now Mohan doesn't know the value of happiness.

Positivity in worst conditions: So, condition is already nastiest, advantageous if you are adverse about it so there is no opportunity of enlightening your condition.

For assistance: Mohan's father has expired, and his Mother is serious.

If he will mislay his state of mind he may lose his mother, if he will think that at least he has a mom to take care of, his father is living a good life now (as explained in Chapter 1).

Positive thinking is the only word we have heard several times.

We advise others to be optimistic. If someone is upset or worried very affectionately we put our aim across their shoulder and ask them to think positive. So, it's a word we believe in and we want to live it. And yet when there is a situation in our own life. Negative or wrong thinking. We call it natural and obvious thinking. Negative thinking in the form of fear and worry.

- Blaming someone or insulting someone
- Feeling jealous when compared with someone
- Competing with someone.
- Feeling hurt when somebody said
- Feeling resentful about someone

It's a wide variety. How to make out whether our thoughts are positive and right? Any thought which annoys my state of mind. If it does not make me feel at ease or uncomfortable. Andrew's ambiances exude to other people and create disturbance in their minds also. That thought is negative. All of us know what negative thinking is. Still, we say, "I didn't want to think that way, but the thought just came." Why does it happen that way when there is a situation. Negative option comes quickly to us? So, we need to understand what is the source of my thoughts...? Thought is our conception. Every thought is energy. But what is the foundation of thought energy?? Why do fewer people create negative thoughts than others? Few people create positive thoughts, and few others create highly preeminent thoughts. Why are we different? And how do I create the right thought? I need to know the source of my thoughts. Thought is energy. What is the raw material that creates the energy? Information is the most important source of thought. It is like a god we eat, is the raw material that gets into the body. Food is the source of energy for the body. It also creates the immunity system of the body. It is based on my diet. That is the reason whenever there is a health issue. The first thing we are told to do is to check our diet and change the diet. Because it's the diet that creates the body. Now, what creates my mind? It is my diet that creates my mind. Which diet? My emotional diet. And what is my emotional diet? Information. Information includes everything that we see, watch and read. All the three get inside. All these three are stored in the mind. They are stored in the subconscious mind and become a part of our thoughts. For many days we have been reading or listening. About an accident or a child traveling on a bike met with an accident and died. if we listen to this news once, twice, or 10 times. For months we have been listening to such information. So that information is fitted into our sub economies minds. Suppose today evening your child does not come home on time. If his phone is out of reach. You don't want to create thoughts about his welfare. You don't want to but you get the thoughts. that he is not in any danger, nothing wrong has happened with him. Why does a wrong thought occur? Why does the mind even worry that something wrong should not have happened? Why does not think something good must have happened, and that is why the child has not come back home. The child must have met somebody or was busy at work, this is why it must have been late. But we think "Hope nothing wrong has happened", "Hope he must not meet with an accident." Does the mind think this way? Because that's the underdone substantial we have fed our mind with. It is all stored in the mind. That several accidents are happening in the world today. So many died on the spot due to accidents. The mind has absorbed that information. So, it will create that thought. So, we need to take care of the information we consume. What we watch, what we read, and what we listen to. Whether we watch a movie. Whether we watch a serial on television. Whether we are eavesdropping on a joke. Whether we are reading a book. Whether we are listening to a song. Very often nowadays driving in-car radio is on. We feel that we are passing time and it's just a song. Every word in that song. The emotions and sentiments in that song are getting recorded in the mind here. We need to remember this is becoming the source of my thoughts. And very soon it will be a part of my vocabulary. Everything that we are hearing. If the mind is feeling low, we prefer listening to sad songs. We don't want to listen to happy songs at that moment. The frequency of our minds at that time is sad and low. Only a sad song carrying a low frequency feels suitable for use inside and that's what matches outside. We need to change our way of thinking. By only changing what we are riveting. Let us take an experiment for just a week. Early morning, instead of wanting to know what is happening in the world. We don't need to listen to it, the first thing in the morning. And that too with visuals. A lot of negative incidents are happening across the world. The media's role is to tell us whatever is happening in the world. The media will not tell us all the rights that are happening in the world. Just in your vicinity, lakhs of people slept peacefully last night. that is not what is going to come into the newspaper. the newspaper will report that last night, there was theft in one house in your area. When they read it once or twice, we start crying... Robbery has amplified so much in today's times. And the fourth time before leaving the house we say, "Lock the house properly, or else a thief might break-in." And very soon we have sown the seeds of fear and anxiety. Just by watching, reading, and listening too much about it. The media will show us what is happening. TV serials, movies, and songs also show a lot of things. A lot is circulated on social media too. What should we consume from them? What should we feed our minds? It's your choice. We start browsing the phone first thing in the morning. Should we fill the mind early in the morning with what is happening around us in the world? Should we fill it with whatever our friends posted last night on social media? What is happening in the world- it's not the first thing to be filled in the morning. First thing in the morning should be pure powerful information. Wisdom, spiritual knowledge, the message of God. We need to fill our minds with the right emotional diet. Thinking will automatically change, and the right thing will automatically change our life. Right now, negative thoughts come automatically. Likewise, pure thoughts will start coming automatically. For that, we need to switch to a pure emotional diet. So, let's take a one-week experiment. For a week we will just listen, read, and watch what we want to be. If I don't want to criticize anybody, I should not watch criticism. Today even senses of humour and jokes are about ridiculing someone or belittling them. We are listening to them and passing time laughing at them. Internally we are becoming like that, and those will start becoming those words. So, let's take a one-week emotional detox. Let's cleanse our mind and soul and thereafter only consume pure information. THEREAFTER WE DON'T HAVE TO WORRY ABOUT POSITIVE THINKING. POSITIVE THINKING AND RIGHT THINKING WILL BECOME A NATURAL WAY OF LIVING.

There are no subtractions and divisions in our mind, there are only addition and multiplication. "I will just remove negative thoughts and I will have positive thoughts."

All the best, it's not going to work. it's just that you need to pay little attention as to how it functions. you will see there is a distinction between what you are and what you gathered. It functions. you will see there is a distinction between what you are and what you have gathered. Well, see the way the question is asked and also the way normally it's addressed is, people think there is something called a negative thought and positive thought. They want to remove the negative thoughts and have only positive thoughts. For such people, I would ask them to just experiment for 10/15 seconds. Let them forcefully remove one thought from their mind.

For assistance: Next 10 seconds, just don't think of a monkey. try not to think of a monkey. You will see you will be full of money. So, what I am saying is, this is the nature of your mind, because, in this mind, all the three pedals are throttle- there is no brake, there is no clutch whatever you touch, it will go faster. In this kind of mind, people have been taught by moral teachers and religious teachers. "Do not think about bad things." Well since then, it's been a full-time job. So, there is no way you can handle your mind like this, this doesn't need any great enlightenment. If you spend two minutes with your eyes closed, you will realize, you cannot do anything forcefully with this mind. So 'I want to remove negative thoughts' do not ever go in this direction because what you want to remove will become your quality, always you will be on it 'So what should I do?' This thing is this- without understanding the fundamental mechanism of this mind because our mind, the human mind is the most sophisticated computer on the planet. Even all the supercomputers have come out like this. When this is the case, is it not important that we understand the mechanics of how it functions? One simplistic aspect of how it functions is- there are no subtractions and divisions in our minds. There is only addition and multiplication. If you try to do something with it, it will say "one more if you try hard, it will multiply into many more to do something with it, it will say "one more" if you try hard, it will multiply into many more. In this mind, you don't try to identify what is positive. what is negative and try to remove it. First of all, one needs to understand, this mind of yours, this body of yours is supposed to serve you. the life you are important. Body and mind are vehicles that must serve us. If you sit in a vehicle, it must go where you want to go. If it goes to its destination, what is the point of such a vehicle? It's just a nuisance. Right now, most human beings are unfortunately experiencing this fantastic possibility of the human mind.

As an exasperation as a misfortune approximately radiant, this is the furthermost stunning entity you have. It's unprejudiced that your prerequisite to reimbursement is slight consecration to its occupations. One unpretentious entity is foremost, and prime process is Meditation. Meditation is something called "you" which exists. This is not an amalgam of all your thoughts and sentiments and physiological process. Beyond that, there is YOU. If you close your eyes, even if you cannot see anything, you're still there. It is through the window of your eyes that you are looking out but if you close your eyes, it doesn't mean that you don't exist, you still exist. So, beyond your thought, you still exist, beyond your emotion you still exist, so that YOU, the life that you are. This has to come into an experience. Why is it that you're not allowing that to come into an experience which is the most significant aspect of who you are? Who you are right now is the most significant aspect is- YOU and ME are alive right now... this is it? 'What I am judicious, what you're judicious is not the imperative thing. We are thriving right now. So, it is vital to prominence on this vital sense of aliveness within you and then you see there is a natural detachment between you and your thought process. Once there is a detachment between your psychological process and your physiological process, this is the end of suffering. Because there are only two kinds of misery that human beings go through- physical misery and mental misery. Once you create a little space between you and your mind and your body, this is the end of misery. This is something every human being has to experience and know otherwise. "I will just remove negative thoughts and I will have positive thoughts "all the best, it's not going to work. One hundred percent it's not going to work, because nobody can remove it, they can avoid it for some time. So, when negative thoughts come you say. Ram Ram Ram or whatever you want bit this is just avoiding it's not gone. The moment you stop that, it will pop back with great force, otherwise, it will arise posterior in your dreams. So, it's very important. First of all, you need to understand- your anger, your resentment, your fear, your anxieties, the negativity that you generate; generally, resentment, anger is always directed towards somebody. But you need to understand this is a poison that we are drinking and expecting somebody else to die. Fortunately, life doesn't work like that. If I drink poison. I die. If I drink poison you don't die. So, we prerequisite to comprehend this. When I Say "poison"-today you can have yourself chemically analysed. Right now, "what is your work? What it says, five minutes of intense anger, check your blood work and see, there will be lots of adverse rudiments in it. You're poisoning yourself. So, do you want to be too toxic yourself? Not. Now the very question is coming from certain helplessness. "What shall I do"? Don't do anything. Sit back and just apprehend yourself with something which is life development. Maybe your heartbeat, maybe your breath, maybe just the sensation of being flourishing. Depending upon how penetrating or how perceptive you are, accordingly, find something, it could be a sensation in the body, it could be breath, it could be a heartbeat, it could be anything, something that indicates life to you. Just pay attention to that for some time. Slowly, you will see there is a distinction between what is you and what you gathered, which includes both your physiological and psychological possibility or mess, whatever you've made out of it.

## HOW TO CONTROL ANGER?

Why do we get angry?? There are few things, few people, our beliefs that we are not leaving that this particular thing is right. So, if anyone says something different, we will get angry. isn't it? Our favourite thing!! Someone is trying to snatch we will get angry. Our greed for something and a hurdle comes between us and that particular thing we will get angry about. Like you are doing a job in a company. and your boss. Just relate whether I am right or wrong. Your boss is materialistic. If he will lose 10 Rupees also, he will respond like he is anguished from a crore rupees forfeiture. if someone is not at all materialistic and someone will steal his 10k even he will be chill!! He will react As an okay blunder happened!! Your boss is an anthropologist. You did a lot of things for him in an authentic way. If he will not extravagance you, you will feel angry… (why he is not getting me). So don't just stick to one image only that you can't lose. If you stick to a particular image, obviously you will be angry. How strongly you will hold anything can be your image or something else… like "I like this gadget" "I like this thing anything else" "it should be done because I like this thing " strong likes and strong dislikes. This is the only root of your anger. isn't it? This is the cause of strong sentiments generated and strong responses. And that strong reaction is out of control, later on, we realize (ab to raita fail gya). So how can it be possible that if an alternative person is crammed out on you, you are avoiding it in (hissy Mazak) Like in the warmth of the moment what response you should give you should be a capability to talk calmly. There are two things. you are fighting with someone with control and second, you don't have control over yourself. Mature souls are the first ones. They boldly say the fact and the second type of person are fighting like nonsense without any logic. now know about the roots of strong likes and dislikes. Dependency is the root of strong likes and dislikes. For example, you are reliant on "this precise is my religion and I am reliant on this ' and when someone will question that you will be angry. Maybe this thing is rubbishing no logic behind it, but you will still be angry. Like by birth you are spoon feed like this you are not leaving any thought. Like this, we are dependent on many things. Now can it happen that we don't depend? IMPOSSIBLE… why? Because till when you are not aware that who you are you are dependable. Why do we depend on a person, a thing, or few thoughts because we are unfilled inside? Like for example "JAIL" those prisoners live in jail when they come, they feel so upset when they go back like in 10/20 or 30 years then they even love that jail too because they were in JAIL for a long time. Now, are you able to see the depth? if you are restrained, tied somewhere you can even start loving that place after a while then we get distressed leaving that too. we get wanted even that environment may not that good and if we talk about Delhi Mumbai (polluted cities) still we love to stay there and in between you go to some hill station for a week in one or two days you will feel like paradise because air is pure there but after one or two days you will miss your city because air may be adulterated there in your cities, but you are customary of that contamination. Like if someone has done a Ph.D. and another one will only call your name you will not feel good to call me doctor and then my name. And you still don't like your job if someone asks what you do on your day. I am working at XYZ company, and you are not happy with that job. even if we go somewhere like to a meditation center when we need someone to tell us how to meditate. We grab that thing and practice it. That time we feel so safe. Everybody who is construal this book please take one day break from your daily routine and do nothing just nothing. What will you get?? I think you will get bored badly. then we will get to know that from inside we feel so empty for filling that emptiness we need few things to do and then we want to unravel our delinquent. It's incredible, totally incredible. but if we look at this truth that is actually what we are? So maybe that truth in which level you are. there is no deficiency in you. you will realize that you want nothing in life that affects you people and problems may come and go you are perfect just perfect. Then nonentity will distress you. This is how you will rethink your antagonism. because nonentity is as imperative as You.

Someone told me that their daughter is just 9 years old and full of annoyance. She terminates belongings in anger. She speaks rubbish at this age only. I had a conversation with that little girl. I asked, "Why do you talk to everyone like this??? If you shout at everyone she said 'I can't control my anger I don't know why I don't like when people go against me'

In her terries, few bricks are around 30. I just said, "do whatever I am saying only for a month because bricks were also 30". Practice supervising your anger daily, just don't try to shout and explain yourself courteously. Do it regularly and keep one brick aside daily from that bundle of 30. I just thought about trying it. She was trying from the next day for two or three days. She was adept but she shouted once or twice a day but from the 4th day she didn't even show her anger, not even once. And in the next 30 days, there was not even one brick. Now she is polite with 1% anger.

Not only this 9 years girl, but even whosoever is reading this can also repeat this. And variety your environs annoyance unrestricted zone. And smile as much as you can.

Some people believe my office table has 8 newspapers. I will read the same news in its newspaper, this sand, then another one, and then finally on the visual screen for visual impact. Its crime, its pain, its trauma which we have overwhelming. We don't have to consume the world's information, we have to take care of our minds and change the world in tomorrow's newspaper. If I keep reading what is in today's newspaper tomorrow's newspaper is going to have more of what it is today's newspaper and that's why if you see even though we are working so hard and trying to change the world issues are only excoriated because we are absorbing it, fashioning it in the mind, bringing it into trauma it intensive by society. Tomorrow's newspaper has more effect so while I am reading I also only read how much it is needed. The second very important thing is the last before you go to sleep because the information I consume last 10 minutes before I sleep will affect my sleep and my 6 hours sleep. The last layer of information has to be pure and clean again. It can be a blessing in love also.

Lately, a girl spoke to me and was irritable about all the glitches, the predicaments, the complications that he was profitable through. She had just lately mislaid her profession for no motive. Her affairs were in a cavernous untidiness. Nobody appreciated her. The whole thing was going erroneously, and he had ended nonentity erroneously. And all concluded the discussion, he set aside enquiring me, "why is this fashionable to me?" I am unquestionable that a lot of you can narrate the state of affairs that this girl was going through. I told her. "Look girl, do what you can do to sort it out if it's your fault to correct it. If it's someone else's fault and that person is within your admittance, deliberate with him. Interconnect to them" very often but, what we conclude is neither our fault nor the fault of someone else. For instance: the serious sickness that we have concluded. We didn't do anything wrong to become it and nonentity experimentalists did anything wrong to have us become it. How do we deal with it? Here's what we do. A little boy once came consecutively to his mother and asked her. "What are you undertaking mom?" she replied, "I am creating a gorgeous, embellished enterprise on this nice textile." The little boy observed up to the fabric, steadily held in the wooden sphere the loop and criticized. A design? All I can see is impartial approximately coloured gossamers- yellow, blue, red, black, pink. All scrambled up, messed up into each other. All hitches! And you call it a strategy? The mother chose a diminutive boy. Put him on her circuit and whispered to him. Now look at it my son and the boy saw a beautiful design. An implausible outline of an organized strategy and an outline embryonic on this fabric. The mother said to the boy. "When you look at fabric from your adjacent, all you see is an untidiness. When you look at the fabric from my side all you see is a stunning design, a pattern, a plan." Dear booklovers, when we conclude the abandoned, irresistible encounters in our life for no fault of ours or no fault of anyone else and we cannot do whatever to sort it out. If we see an immoral appearance from our theme of view, all we see is a mess. All we see is a state of affairs and measures scrambled, jumped up to generate that mess. But when we look at the equivalent state of affairs from life's fact of interpretation, from god's point of view. We see a beautiful design, a pattern, a plan embryonic in our lives. In fact, for a good-looking strategy of sewing to materialize on one side, you cannot evade the mess on the further side. And it's not impartial to the countryside of embroidery, such as the countryside of life as well. This viewpoint essentially stretches us a very deep sagacity of innermost forte and resilience to the appearance of such abandoned, devastating encounters in our life. MODIFICATION OF YOUR VISUALIZATION AND YOUR VISUALIZATION WILL CHANGE YOU!!

## ONE ENTITY TO REMINISCE WHEN THE WHOLE THING ENTHUSIASMS ERRONEOUS

We are going through life in the mode we are facing, not because that's how life is, but because that's how we are. Our involvement in life is in essence strong-minded by us, not by what's trendy from place to place. There is the status quo in the world, intimate, exertion, street, many things, anti-monopoly, all varieties of status quo. Whatever transpires in the detached state of affairs has a convinced quantity of influence on our corporeal survival, indisputably it has, doesn't it? But it does not govern the countryside of our involvement. The countryside of our involvement is contingent on how we are. State of affairs and progression is dependent on millions of other individuals. Your life is status quo right now. Existing in Kolkata, what every inhabitant of Kolkata is responsible for has approximately influence on your peculiar status quo, but its prerequisites do not have any influence on your involvement in life, as your involvement in life is fundamentally strong-minded by you, you, and you alone, averageness investigational but you. If you comprehend this, that is the foundation of sadhana. You are sedentarily miserable with your eyes closed, impartial to comprehend experientially that the whole thing that I involve is imminent from within me. Agony and gravity are approaching from within you, delight and unhappiness are approaching from within you, anguish and trance are fashionable from within you. If you comprehend this much then would you indicate agony or preference? Would you take happiness or desolation? Anguish or trance? That's all you identify as excellent. If you are disordered about the choice. Then you would prerequisite a lot of instructions. Your high quality is vibrant, for yourself. 100% clear. so, when it is so vibrant, excellent is vibrant, the only entity is your capability to variety optimal. That's all your requirement to expand. If you did not identify what to indicate, it would be more intricate. Your prime is 100% vibrant, only to be intelligent to take. That's what sadhana is approximate. Not about bringing up the rear, not about accomplishing it spinally. That you can indicate what ought to transpire within you precisely now. Desolation or enjoyment? Distress or trance? Discomfort or preference? What should transpire in this? You are the solitary person who is influential in this, but you know, occasionally if you're despondent, you get something. Right from infantile you've been proficient in corresponding to this. If you act despondent, somebody will attend to you. You will get convinced. As a child you were despondent; your mother gave you two extra seagulls that demonstrated approximately in your concentration. If I am despondent, I will get what I want. But if you are despondent, whatever you get, what's the opinion? Yes? Once you're despondent, whatever you get. What is your opinion? If you're ecstatic, you don't get anything so whole the hell cares. Stop sensation despondent.

Are you to come until your life is unruly unrestricted to be content? If so, you could be to come for an extensive stretch like persistently. The idea that you can't be content except and pending some disorder is met can itself be an enormous fence to contentment. While it is unquestionably usual to require that a history of infrequent anxiety would be concluded, you might be behind a lot of exclusive life by philanthropic disproportionate desolation and unpleasantness. I am not portentous that you counterfeit happy your way over the day. Within your stimulating milieu. I am portentous that you treasure real happiness. If only for a few transcripts at the time of sequence, if you are sensation miserable, out of the regulator, or suicidal. Please pursue help. Recognize the misery you are undergoing, investigate specifies that long-suffering your undesirable frame of mind will, illogically, intensify your well-being. Long-suffering undesirable frames of mind such as disenchantment, annoyance, and despondency will also condense anxiety. While it is not clear why acceptance of an adverse state of mind is such an effective stratagem, the aforementioned examination has revealed that cataloguing adverse state of mind. "I am resentful" "this is despondency" etc. alterations the sensitivity demonstrative fragment of your intelligence to the discerning fragment of your intelligence. Once your "philosopher" is on boarding, you can put your state of mind in perspective. Proposal by handsome empathy. Conversation friendly too by hand could bring instant of cosiness. You may not have numerous people in your life accurate now who can give you the profound sympathy that you need, but you do have one person that is you., give yourself authorization you be content when conceivable. Communicate yourself that you don't prerequisite to sensation embarrassed for wanting instants of liberation, contentment, and delight in your life. Involvement in good-looking and vigorous disruptions. Once you authorize yourself to be happy, you can better allow yourself the involvement of unimportant preferences. A place, a cup of coffee, and a visit to the park. Remind yourself that it's ok to have fun, even assuming a portion of your life is deteriorating away from each other.

## WHEN COMPLICATIONS ARE BEYOND OUR RESISTOR

It was a scorching straw-hat day in Mumbai. One of those days when the clamminess is so from top to toe, that your perspiration is irrational. I categorically chose some renewed, cool lemonade for myself. As I instigated, a friend of mine called and in the process of speaking to her, I didn't appreciate that I made a big error. I ended up accumulating about 5 times the expanse of lemon to the water than what was desirable. God, it was so sour that one sip dispensed into the mouth of a cataleptic man would probably bring him back to perception. Well, somehow or the other, I had to precise this now and as much as I wanted to eradicate some lemon juice out of the water to make it taste perfect again, it was incredible. Because SOME THINGS IN LIFE CAN JUST NEVER BE UNDONE. There was no way to eradicate the extra lemon from the water but there sure would be a way to inject the tricky. The only way to exact the status quo was to add four spectacles of water and dilute it. And here I was as a substitute for one, now I had 5 glasses of fresh lemonade ready to be served out of 4 more people. And I think life is the same. Occasionally we cannot undo some things that may have gone wrong in our life. SOME WRONG DECISIONS, WRONG CHOICES, WRONG INVESTMENTS, WRONG WORDS that we have articulated can never be concluded. Not that we shouldn't try. We should undeniably give our very best. But after partaking, doing what we can, when we cannot inverse things to still preserve, trying is like endeavouring to eradicate lemon from water and I think that would be such a sheer waste of time. As a substitute, we should try to exertion on ADDING SO MANY RIGHT THINGS IN OUR LIFE THAT THE WRONG SEEMS SMALLER THAT WHAT IT WAS EARLIER. When complications seem to be dependent elsewhere our control. Moderately than basically annoying to eradicate them, let us ADD POSITIVITY IN OUR LIFE AND CHANGE OUR EXPERIENCE.

## WHY AND HOW TO FINISH THE EXPECTATIONS?

What is the connotation of expectancy? I expected ABC to wear a snowy t-shirt and he would be dressed in red. Is it ordinary for me to have that anticipation? I can have or not have been not imperative. I am tolerable to expect but whether he will accomplish my expectancy or not. I didn't tell him I was just expecting him to wear a white t-shirt. How many times are you telling people everything? If I say to ABC "why couldn't you do this copious thing for me?" now my opinion will be "visualize he could not uniform wear one white t-shirt for me just see. "I don't like red" "and now most imperative you know I don't like for wearisome read" "you know what I am in pain" and the most imperative ordinary credence classification "you are the origin of my pain" scrupulously this is the one-line cause of the inconsistent association. Sounds so funny right now. right? Why is it funny because its conference is so ill common-sense that how could you assume him to wear silvery? Just to be able to understand if you find me expecting him to wear a white t-shirt wrong, just sit one day and scan your potentials. We are not expecting people to only wear cloth in our way, we are expecting them to be our way. When they cannot wear one shirt colour my way. Why would somebody be my way? Most imperative, am I ready to be there? So, he can just look back and say, "why don't you just wear a red dress? This is what we do every day with each other. Why should I meet his/her expectancy?" Why should I be the way you want to be? Why can you variation the way I am? Simple one credence system which starts generating skirmish and struggle and conflict. Every time there will be conflict, we check to instigate there will be the credence system because it is so strong inside anticipation is ordinary. Huge modification on anticipation is ordinary to its problems. We can do it. Just pause and convey to people next to you whether it's your spouse, brother, sister, whether it's with the people you function with how they can be? Who do I want them to be? How is it conceivable? Suppose one day two or four in a family wake up in the morning and they are all indistinguishable. Now that's also humorous. We are diverse. That's also funny but envision now that's what we want to contemplate like be, be like me, or perform like me. So, one morning my whole family wakes up and thinks the same, they perform the same. Is it fine? We want that. Is it fine? Why is it not fine? Because we have concluded that this credential system's prospects are not bad. Is it ordinary for people to like diverse colours? Normal? Is it normal for people to like different foods? Different songs? Movies? Book? Very basic possessions even there we are not analogous. And here we want them to deliberate like me. Be like me. Have the same empathy as me. How many of you like flowers? I don't like flowers I hate them. Is it okay? Is it okay? Sure? Booklovers everyone approved? Why does anybody like the precise thing? I may abhor that thing. What we have to do is the shift from an involuntary way of existing where we don't pause before we contemplate, we don't hiatus previously we judge, we don't pause to resolve whether this is right or erroneous. You like flowers, most of you like flowers, most of you the world like flowers. So does that mean if somebody does not like flowers it is not right? It's all about fluctuating the training just contemplating if someone doesn't like flowers is that okay? They may be hypersensitive to it so maybe intelligent for a rational purpose because they don't like flowers. I am not allowed to like it if I am not allergic to it. Okay. I am not sensitive to it. But I don't like analogous flowers. Is that okay? Who is right, you or me? Both are right in their way, none of us is wrong. Only because they are diverse from us, we can just go home think, have faith in and appreciate and say you were also precise I was also right there will not be any solitary struggle in any affiliation because that struggle is all about, I am precise, and you are erroneous, and the other person will say I am right and you are erroneous. And there we are scorching disrespect. Believing that reverence is the underpinning of affiliation but every time I create this thought I am right you are wrong I am scorching insolence I am radiating rejection and now if you create a thought for me that how can I not like flowers? I can create a thought for you what is there in this to like I am not understanding. And so, you and I start deriding each other's choice and start calling each other. How can you be like this? This is the cordial cast-off. And we say that we want to be unconditionally affectionate. It is incredible to love somebody unconditionally if anticipation is normal in your life. Because somewhere someday some instant there will be not meet up to my expectancy and when they do not meet up to my prospect, I will grow wounded and when I will get hurt I will cast-off and say I am not tolerant. So categorical acceptance is just a nice word. And a lot of denunciation is what is fashionable today. We keep saying to each other "I love you." How many times in a day do we have to say I love you to each other now every phone call ends with I love you. Every message ends with I love you. Do we need to say it so many times, but we need to say it alteration that today we want to say it again and again then let's start the proverb I accept you? Say it 20 times in a day after every phone call, after every message, after every conversation. I accept you. And if I say 20 times a day after erstwhile, I shift from anticipation to receipt. What we have just done is accepted each other. That your right and my right is diverse. It's not precise and erroneous it's two diverse rights. And why two individuals are diverse, why individuals can't have the same likes and dislikes. Why are they different? Depending on their environment, depending on their childrearing, contingent on their instruction, ethnic group, philosophy and so many things people are going to be diverse. Now all these influences we are seeing only one lifetime. A piece of unity for us. And that's why religiousness gives the reaction.

Science has to immobile find out. Devoutness says I AM ON A JOURNEY. Today I AM IN THIS COSTUME, PREVIOUS TO THIS ANOTHER COSTUME AFTER THIS ANOTHER COSTUME readers how many of you have two children? Or more than two? How many of you have two children indistinguishable with disposition and have you ever pause and think why you have two children differently. Same parents, same country, mostly same school, same environment, same friends, same the whole thing. Then why are these two children different? One can be afraid, reclusive while the other is smiling. Can one be self-assured? Fearful. Why are they so different? Then parents say I have given them the whole thing, why are they so diverse? When was that modification created? Even parents have given indistinguishable rearing to both of them. Because their parents have seen it only after they come into this costume. So, their present influences are all indistinguishable but before they enter into the womb of the mother that they were in another costume, another costume meant another family, another environment. Before that alternative one, before that another one. We are only 30/40/50 in this costume before that 100 and another 100 and another one. So, it's like a CD with so many recordings of at least 500/2000/200000 years so many songs, and one day two CDs get married so if your CD is sedentary next to you have a look. Another soul and this soul, two souls, completely different recondense of many years and one day they get married and they look at each other and say how can you be like this? You are so strange the other person says even you are very strange. And then starts a journey of trying to copy my song into another CD. Please be like this for me just for my sake become like this. Why do we need to entreat people to become another way for us? Why are we standing Infront of everybody and saying please be the way I want you to be? Is this called long-suffering, regarding and loving people? no. and why are we annoying to copy our song to another CD? One or two years and a third CD came into our family and for 9 months they both were thinking they were going to get a blank CD. And both of them have had nice conversations for 9 months. For the reason that we thought it will blank the CD and we will facsimile songs conferring to us, and I am indisputable none of you got a blank CD. No. so one more CD and you will say how can you be like this? And sometimes a child's samskaras are entirely different from their parents so each one of us has five folders of sinkers. If we understand those five folders. It is very easy to understand each other. There cannot ever be a misinterpretation in that.

1. Which I transmit from my past.

2. Which I become from my family

3. Environment

4. Will power

This binder is communal for each one as the previous dossier is diverse for every person, parental will be diverse for everybody, and uniform in brethren two children will get different samskaras from their parents they are not profitable to take same samskaras from the parents. Even in the parental binder, they are going to choose what they take. This is common to everyone that is the original Sanskars of every soul. No soul on this planet does not have this Sanskar. Sankar- peace. Does everybody like peace? Yes. Even those who are doing things that are not peaceful. And then when you ask why you are doing this, they will say I need peace. Methods could be a question mark but what they want is peace so peace, love, happiness, purity, power, knowledge, bliss are the seven Sanskars.

One inventive folder which every soul has. And when we look at an additional soul with this empathetic feeling that this soul is the pure soul authoritative soul diplomatic soul contented personality but right now, they are using some Sanskar from their other four folders. We can respect every soul for who they are. And most importantly we can start helping each other to galvanize their innovative folder Sanskars now where is the Sanskar of antagonism folder? Where is the Sanskar of annoyance and where is the Sanskar of peace? Sankar of peace is in my innovative binder and Sanskar of annoyance is in the parental or environment of my past but because I am using it too much that's why my Sanskar has come into my unconscious way of living so we say this is ordinary. So, we don't have faith that we are creating it. Like someone says "we don't do it, it's just materializing" when we are saying it's just happening that means Sanskars go into mechanical mode not cognizant mode. I don't intentionally imagine. Opportunities impartially materialize. Now, what do we have to do? What is religiousness? To start opening the 5th folder. And to start using the Sanskar of the 5th folder more often till within a few days the 5th folder will go into automatic mode.

## EMPHASIS ON YOURSELF, NOT OTHERS

It's the very corporate impression. And I reckoned out why that is, I think. So, conceive that we previously know from an experimental viewpoint that, if you set out an earlier towards an objective, which do you want to do because your essential aim you need a track. Because that provides you with a constructive sentiment. Accurate? So, you usually up rather as appreciated. That suggests grading. You set up something that is appreciated. You choose that you're going to do that in its place of additional things so that's generous of detriment because you're forfeiting entirety else to chase that. And then your involvement a reasonable minute of optimistic reaction and meaning as you timepiece yourself more towards the objective. And so, the inference of that is that the better that goal, the bursting supplement your skill is going to be when you follow it. So that's one of the motives for emergent an idea and for fleshing yourself out theoretically because your intention at peak objective that you can accomplish. Ok, so you organize that. And then you'll find is that as you transfer towards the goal there are confident things that you have to finish that terrify you. You know, maybe you have to acquire to be a restored orator or a better journalist or better intellectual. You have to be recovering the people everywhere around you or you have to absorb some new assistance and you're anxious about that whatever because it's going to elasticity you if you try an aim. So that's put you up against experiments. So, all the proven data signposts, well, the contrary of non-toxic galaxies, as Jonathan hadith has been aiming out, that what you want to do when you recognize something that someone is evading that they prerequisite to do because they're frightened. You help them willingly oppose it. And so, you disrupt it, depressed, what you try to do if you're a psychoanalyst, as you break down the thing they're ducking into reduced and minor fragments until you find a piece small enough thus, they'll do it. And it doesn't trouble as long as they start it, you know, then they can put the next piece on in the next piece. And what chances are they don't get less anxious, faithfully? They get pluckier. It's like there's extra of them. And here's why you envision yourself doing something new. And that's revealing, right? There are statistics in the exploit and then you can integrate that evidence and turn it into dexterity and fit into a revolution of your views. So, there's further to you. Because you've taxed something innovative. So that's one article. The second thing is there's a good organic indication for this now that if you put yourself in a new condition, then a new genetic factor, a program for new proteins and build new unbiased structures and new nervous system constructions. Something happens to some gradation when you work out, right? Because your forces are retorting to the short, but your nervous system does that, too. So, you envisage that there's a lot of impending you locked in your heritable cipher. And if you put yourself in a new condition, then the anxiety, that's the situational trauma that's produced by that certain position, exposes those genetic factors, and then figures new portions of you. And so that's very calm because who knows how much there is shelter exclusive of you. Ok, so now here's the inkling. So, let's adopt the gauges as you take on thicker and weightier heaps that more and more of you, you get more and more informed because you're doing more and more challenging things. But more and more of you get cracked. And so, then what would denote that if you got to the point where you could look at the riskiest thing so that you would be the chasm, right? If you could look at the lenient things, like the most vicious parts of the misery of the world and nastiness of people and humanity. You could keep a look at that conservative and unswervingly, that they would turn you hugely. So that's the idea of rescuing your father because envision that you're like the probable merged of all your all the inherited insight that's sealed inside of you geologically. But that's not going to come out at all without you hassle yourself unless you task yourself. And the superior you challenge to take on the more that's going to chance on. And so that as you take in an expansive range of experiments. And you push yourself as a soldier, then more and more of what you could be tried on. And that's corresponding to transmuting yourself into their inherited father, into all because you're like they would you call it? You're the significance of all these existing organisms that have come before you. And that's all part of your biotic potentiality. And if you can push yourself, then all of that clicks on and that turns you into who you could be. That's and that's the symbol of that affirmative familial father. The point is, your best tactical situation is how am I deficient and how can I remedy that? That's what you've got. And the thing is, you are inadequate. And you could cure it, both of those are within your grab if you aim low enough. That's another thing you keep saying. Ambition low enough have low enough saloon. For example, you got a toddler, and you want the adolescent to expand. You don't set them a slab that's so high that it's incredible for them to conquer it. You take a look at the kid, and you reflect, ok these kids got this range of dexterity. Here's a challenge we can fling at him or her that outstrips their modern level of expertise, but gives them a practical prospect of realization. And so, like I am adage it tongues in bravery to some gradation, you know, it's like. But if you're but I am doing it as a supporter of humbleness. It's like I don't know how to start cultivating my life. Someone might say that I would say, well. You're not targeting stumpy enough. There's something you could do that you are regarding as probationary. That you could do, that you would do that would result in a genuine perfection. But it's not a big enough improvement for you, so you won't lower yourself enough to take the opportunity. Incremental ladders.

## HOW TO CONTEMPLATE FEWER AND MORE ACCURATELY?

When we rehearse piety. When we consider this, we will grasp that the life cycle is very relaxed. Everything is very calm. It is a way to take care of health, to keep an affiliation plan. It is very relaxing to remain unchanging whenever there is an encounter in life. We would feel prior that it is very trying, but it is very easy. But to swing everything from being difficult to easy when being the only thing we were hypothetical to do? Whatever is taking care of everything else, we just need to take care of it. Who has to annoy every passage of life? "I" right? It is "I". Who generates our associations? "I". Who is persuading our health? "I" who is taking care of our work or business? "I" if there is a task in that workshop or commercial whole will handgrip it? "I" if there is an issue in the family, who will take care of it? It's like you have a certain thing that will do every mission in your lifecycle. "I" everything is going to transpire from the "I". But that "I" saying- I don't have time for myself. It's like you have something which will do every chore in your life. Everything. Name anything in your life and it is that I have to do it. How much should we highlight? How much do we abbeys "I"? Today even considering a handset a phone does a lot of our responsibilities. That is the reason we don't authorize the house in the morning without arranging it. We say- it's my receiver. How can I leave the house without alleging it, because how will we manage throughout the day without charging the headset? We want to go from one place to the other. We use GPS on our phones. Of course, other things like calls, messages, and emails. Listening to songs, inspecting videos, ticking photos, shopping online, booking tickets. The majority of work is trendy through the phone itself. Do we ever forget to charge the receiver? No, because we know that we cannot complete our responsibilities throughout the day without charging the phone. But who is the one using that phone? "I" who is the one using that phone? There is a useful object, but putting it to good use. I have a good phone but if I don't know half of its features, then I am not using it. So, the "I" is not furnished to use it right. So, the "I" should be proficient. But by continually saying and range it is becoming a mutual line. That- I don't have time. One person must have said it sometime. People who caught him must have said- it sounds pleasant and accurate. Actually, where do I have the time? So, within a few days 5 more people started to say it. It is like in schools where one child says something and 5 others don't have time, I don't have time. We will find time lacking in our life. Now the question is- don't we have time, or don't we have power? When we need to do a task, the "I" should have the power to do it. Isn't it? Today the "I" is taking longer or more time to complete any task. It is taking us more time to finish tasks. Because when this "I" gets ready to begin the work. A lot of other things are going on or within it. Your something was going was something going on. Something happened just before you left. So physically you have switched from home to work. But that "I go to both places"- your work and your home. Because it is not physical. Despite being at the workplace it can visit your house. Or being at your home it can visit your workplace. So at any point in time, it is doing multiple things. So wherever it should remain and whatever it should think. When it does not do it. If someone says something to me, I need to finish all the matter with one thought. I should be able to think- so what if I said it? It won't make a difference to me. As a substitute today I am creating 10 thoughts. How may perhaps they say it, why did they say it, no matter how hard I work they keep saying such things. We kept on thinking. How many thoughts were we supposed to spend on that matter? Just one. How many thoughts do we way? The task which is supposed to finish with one thought. The task is getting stretched. It can go on for 1 hour and beyond. We are doing some other work, but that topic is going on in the background. It's not that we are just sitting and thinking about it. We have switched over to the next task. But in the background, that same topic is going on. What about the of "I"? It obviously reduces. We feel that we are working on something else. We are working on some other tasks, but you are not working on them at 100% efficiency. because internally, we were thinking of approximately the same thing simultaneously. So, when we are doing some tasks. And our 100% is not going into the task. And if the quality of the thought going on in the background is not very nice. What happens to the quality of thought created in response to the present situation? It will be low quality. Because n=energy the background is not a good quality. If someone said something. My mind is thinking about it. And some situation unfolds in front of me. I am hypothetical to respond to that situation with my best energy. But a negative song is playing in the background. So, the chances of creating the right response reduce slightly. Subsequently, there will be an effect of one situation on the next situation. And the effect of that situation on the next situation. It continues that way because it is going on here in my mind. So the energy of one scene enters the next scene. The energy of the subsequent passage goes to the third scene. Since how many days is it going on? If we look at ourselves like a detached spectator, look at ourselves being detached in what state of mind we are doing such big errands of life. We are doing major errands. But our municipality of cognizance is not precise. Because we have not given the power and practice to the mind. What to think in this situation and how soon to finish the matter. When it comes to the doing- which means by when should this task be completed? We fix that easily and say – I will complete it In 30 minutes. But we don't fix how long we need to think about this work. So there is never a lack of time for anything. It is only the lack of energy. The more our mind is emotionally weak the longer we will need to complete a task. How do we make out whether our mind is weak or powerful? It is decided whether- my mind influences the situation, or the situation influences my state of mind. Which of these is true? Does my mind influence the situation? Or does the situation influence me? Do I influence other people or do other people influence me? Which is true> let's take an example of a situation. Is my state of mind, my choice? Or is it dependent on this situation? Mental emotional power depends on what you choose. But the situation is in front of us. In this situation, how should I feel? Is it my choice or does it depend on how the situation is? Okay, let's do one thing. Close your eyes for a minute, reader. Bring on the screen your mind any situation that happened this week, where your mind got slightly disturbed. There was some incident, or you were in a certain situation? Where did your mind get slightly disturbed? There were two things- one was the situation and the other was my state of mind. Now we need to check. Was my disturbed state of mind caused by the situation? Or is my state of mind independent of this situation? That no matter what the situation is, my state of mind is my choice. And is it possible that in the same situation, my mind could have persisted calm and stable? Not distressed in the same circumstances. In the equivalent circumstances which you saw now. One answer is problematic. The second response is possible. At least you said it is possible, that is a big thing. Whether it is difficult or easy is secondary. If you had said impossible then there would be no point even trying. First, we need to be clear who is influencing whom? This is the situation. This is my state of mind. Who is more powerful? The mind should be powerful? It's not about what "should be powerful. In reality, what is powerful? Circumstances or my state of mind? State of mind. If we don't pay attention to this, right now we will ay-situation was like that, so I got worried. We have been axiom this line for a very long while. When the situation was pleasant I was happy. It's time we repeat this line, what programming are we strengthening on the mind? This is being precise by this. We are repeating this line. We say –there was so much traffic that irritation was apparent. What they said was so wrong, that feeling bad was natural. They did not complete the given task, so getting angry was obvious. My child failed in exams, so feeling hurt was natural. Each line Is reinforcing the software design. What is programming? That what goes on here in the mind-how I think, how I feel, how I speak, how I behave. Which means me. The "I"- what did I become dependent on? On situations. Since how long? We don't even know. Today it has become so dependent on the status quo that we say it is apparent, it's ordinary. We say- as is the situation, so will be my mood. We started saying this equation is right. Situations will not be as per my choice. We suppose approximately, but the status quo will turn out to be entirely diverse at this period. We expect the other person to speak in a certain way. But he will speak in a completely different manner. We don't even have to go too far. Even people who live at home. We expect a particular behaviour from them. But they suddenly behave in a completely different manner. So how many situations do we face throughout the day? Scene after scene after scene. Just detach yourself and look at what programming you have created in your mind. Throughout the day, scene after scene there is a situation. And we programmed my state of mind. Is dependent on this situation. The scene changes every few minutes. Sometimes good, sometimes not. Sometimes excellent, sometimes too bad. It fluctuates. And we said my mind is dependent on the situation. So what happens to my mind throughout the day? It keeps fluctuating. When I feel my mind is dependent on the situation. But I want to be happy. So I believed the situations in my life should be perfect. So we created a simple formula for "I". "I" is reliant on one situation. We disbursed most of our life this way. Today the status quo is more changeable. Until the time when the status quo was more or less persistent and pleasing. Even though we had made "I" dependent on the status quo. That "I" was more or less satisfactory. We intentional, became a gradation, got into a profession. Entities said- now they are innocuous. That we were nonviolent pending we give up work from our jobs. The mind was also innocuous. The job was nonviolent, the mind was also innocuous. Today we don't recognize it. Even if we don't misplace our job, our mind distinguishes that we can lose it anytime. So, the mind has developed contingent on an object which is in jeopardy. We can lose any time. Showing the anxiety and self-doubt in the mind started fetching persistently. Noe even if we haven't lost the profession, the anxiety and uncertainty are immobile contemporaries. Because what are the statistics here? That whatsoever can occur at any time. Disappeared are the epochs when a person would get blood heaviness or any other illness after the age of 60 or 70. Today we are saying anything can happen, anytime. Gone are the times when after marriage, the couple will stay together for a lifetime. Again we say- anything can happen anytime. So when situations were more or less normal. At that time, even if the mind was dependent on this situation. It would still be normal and fine. But now that situation has become so variable. And if we make our mind depends on a variable just see how variable the mind has ongoing appeal. So, what happens to mind supremacy? Its sanctuaries flutter between high and small. So, what materialized the power of the mind? It started diminishing. And the more stimulating the situation started, since the concentration was at the forgiveness of that status quo, it started diminishing even more. Now let us check the equivalence itself. We said- they did like that, so I got apprehensive. They did not complete the task, so I got fuming. Circulation was so high I got annoyed. My child was ill so apparently, I was worried. This is one way of living. Alternative means of living is- no matter how much road traffic there is, my mind is stable. My child is ill, but I am constant. They did not comprehensive the mission, so I recommended them. But I am constant. Somebody said something not very pleasant, it demonstrates their nature. I am stable. Is it conceivable to live like this? It is not even about whether it is conceivable. It is about what is veracity. What is the veracity? Supposing this is the status quo. This can be the status quo in my life, as I can generate 10 thoughts about this flower container. Can I not generate any thoughts? I can. So, presume this is our status quo in life. It is not compulsory that state of affairs requirements be immense. This can be a state of affairs. Just twitch discerning about it. Whatever we contemplate and sensation about this. Who does it contingent on? In the same condition- which is the flowerpot-if each of us needs to create 5 thoughts about it. This is just one flowerpot, which means the situation is the same. Will all of us create the same 5 thoughts about it? Well, think about it. We had situations that were equal to feelings. The situation is the same so all of our thoughts should be? This is a situation of life that has come in front of us. It is the same situation in front of all of us. All of us get stuck in the same traffic jam. 100 employees have the same boss who solders them the same way for the same error. Everybody's children fall ill sometime or the other. So, most situations in life are nearly equal for everyone. But each person's response and thoughts in the same situation are going to be diverse. An important person can become very hyper in the same situation. ill hyper, there will be a bit hyper. Someone else will be calm. And another will be very diplomatic. The situation has not changed for anyone. Tough. If it is true that the mind is dependent on the situation. Then in the same situation, how should all of our minds be? We should have the same state of mind. So today I dewdrop this erroneous equivalence at this withdrawal center that my mind is reliant on. This one equivalence is the purpose for all life's skirmishes. Because we said as is the situation. So is my state of mind. And we exhausted our supremacy.

## DON'T FASTENER PEOPLE'S DEMONSTRATIVE CONTAMINATION

God teaches us a beautiful line. Criticism and appreciation are to be treated equally, as the same. People might appreciate us. People might appreciate us a lot. When someone appreciates us, what are they reflecting? Have you experienced anytime, that you are the same? But someone appreciates you a lot. Someone says you are very nice. And someone might say you are horrible. Someone says I can spend my whole life with you. Someone else says I cannot put up with you for an hour. We are the same person. Do we people have so many different opinions about us? Because that opinion is contingent on them. Every time we have to remember this. So, if someone appreciates us, it is reflecting their state of mind. If you remember that when somebody appreciates you. That whoever is appreciating me, at this it is reflecting their Sanskar. Do not say- I am good is what they said. If we think that they are calling us good, it means we have consumed their appreciation. If we consume appreciation, we cannot escape consuming criticism. And then what happens? We will fluctuate both in appreciation and in criticism. And if we keep fluctuating throughout the day, our inner power will keep depleting. So, when somebody appreciates me, it is shimmering their state of mind. And when somebody criticizes me, it is reflecting their state of mind. Take feedback from people but not the liveliness of criticism. Both are very different. One is feedback and one is the energy of criticism. Suppose this is a table and I want to give feedback on this. So, I can say This tablecloth is not very clean today. It should be better tomorrow. This is feedback. The energy of criticism will be they always keep it dirty do whatever you want but there is no cleanliness here. No idea what they do throughout the day. Can't they clean the tablecloth? Don't consume this energy. Because this energy is of no use to you. What is useful to you is just that one line of feedback. Whose Sanskar is the energy of criticism? It's my state of mind. Just take your feedback but don't consume my energy. Because if you consume my energy as a critic. That was my emotional illness. If we say they spoke like this to me. It is not true that they spoke like that to me. Today their mind is disturbed. Keep the energy there. Because if we consume other people's energy which is not healthy. The first one was ill but after that? It is like if 5 people live in a house one of them returns home in the evening, feeling a little unwell. He had a cough and cold. By the next morning, another person at home also fell ill. That person will not admit that his immunity system is weak. He will say you passed on your illness to me. Vocabulary is very important. Because every time we say you are the one who gave this to me it means that has nothing to do with me. Every time we blame someone else for how we are thinking and feeling we are giving up our emotional strength. The need of the hour is to be emotionally self-governing. Demonstrative independence means whatsoever is getting created here is completely my choice. The situation is here. It could be good or may not be good. It could be favourable, a crisis, chaos, or anything. That's the energy of the situation.

What I will create in my mind is completely my choice. In the same situation, will five people create the same thoughts? No. But the situation was the same. if situations are creating our thoughts. Then one situation should create the same response in all five people. Today if we talk about all the readers, the situation is the same for us. But feelings in Everyone will be different. So, the situation is not creating your feelings. You're looking at the situation and creating your feelings. So emotional independence means never to say I am feeling like this because of (anything outside). Each time we say because of… because of. because of…, we imply that where is the remote control of this mind? With other people so other people had a choice. If they pressed this button, you were happy. If they pressed the other button, you were down. The situation can harm us financially. The situation can harm us professionally, the situation can harm us physically. We are talking emotionally. Because all these things are outside.

Body, career, money- they all are outside. So what is external can be only harm by external things. What about inside? Nobody can get inside here. The situation can harm your throat. But how upset you should be because of it. How angry you should be. Whether you speak lovingly, angrily, or shout at someone. Should you scream only a little a lot? All these pronouncements are made privileged. For that, we are not going to blame the situation. For the reason that when we start blaming the situation for what we are feeling here. Then our self is not in our control anymore. Our life goes out of our resistor. Life is not what emerges to us. Life is how we re-join to what happens to us. Life is not about situations that come into our life. The status quo is not in our resistor. What is in our resistor? How we think about that situation. How we speak in that situation. How we behave in that situation. If we are in our resistor, life will be beautiful. In some people's life, everything is going perfectly well, outside. But they are not happy inside. They will find something wrong even if everything is fine. And there are also people in whose life nothing is going right at this time. But they are doing very fine. Ask them how life is, and they will say it is beautiful. Even if you remind them that they have so many problems, they will say- so what? Because they are perfect inside. We don't need this to be faultless. (Peripheral status quo) we need this to be faultless (interior situation. some people will have 100- degree fever. And they will be suffering accurately, because of a slight fever. And some people will have a chronic illness. Even in that stage, they remain very bright and easy, and they annoyed it. So, what is the size of the illness? And what is the size of the anguish? It is categorical in my mind. If we want to finish all these emotional illnesses. We only have to become emotionally independent. Because if we hold situations and people responsible for how we are thinking and feeling then each time the situation is not my way. I will react. And respectively time I react, what happens to my energy? It decreases. There will be another situation and again it will decrease. And then another situation and yet again it will decrease. So, what happened to my inner power? It kept depleting. When it kept dappling, I started getting disturbed even in a small scene. That is anxiety. And we reach a stage where we don't need a situation. When there is absolutely no situation, and everything is perfect which means the battery is depleting. So, one equation which needs to be fitted His inner world is not dependent on the outer world. The inner world is dependent on me. So, what we need to do is that in all small scenes that keep coming throughout the day when you are saying I am angry because of… I am angry because of…. I am irritated because of… I am happy because of… I just need to take my finger back and say I am angry because of how I reacted. Now I will change my thoughts. Most people around us are going through one or the other emotional illness. Can you see those emotional illnesses? What emotional illnesses do you see around you? Depression is not an emotional illness. It is a mental health issue. That's an illness that needs dealing with. What are the emotional viruses you see? Short temperateness in people around us. They have that illness, how will they behave? Yes, they will be a little distressed. No problem. What else? Irritability is an illness. Frustration is an illness.

Criticism is an illness. This means no matter how well you work, I have the illness of criticism. So, what will I say? It has nothing to do with you, your work, and your efficiency. I am not well. But if you are going to work so hard. And then just expect one word of appreciation. You didn't get that appreciation anyway. Instead, you got criticism. And if you consume that? So, we will have to see people who are not well around us. And when we see people who are not well. What feelings do we create for them when we know that they are not well? Empathy. Until now what feeling did we have? Anger… so shift why do we get angry at them? Because we think they said this to me.

But now we understand, they are sad and they are ill. So, what can we do for them? When somebody is physically ill, we take care of them. Now we need to take care of those who are emotionally ill.

For assistance: I had a conversation with the nurse she was miffed I asked what happened? She said doctors scold me anytime, anywhere even in front of patients also I feel so bad. I saw what about patients? She said they also throw plates, don't have a meal, and shout but I don't feel bad because they are ill. see patients are ill physically and what about doctors? Mentally stressed.

The next day nurse sneered when the doctor shouts and said sorry please be calm and take care. Then she said it is very simple. Religiousness prompts us that each one is a passion on a diverse expedition.

Resounding different Sanskars. Someone has suspiciousness and someone who has diffidence has empathy for them. When you are on responsibility and if someone gets incapacitated, you put your life discourse and save them why don't you leave them there? You will never do that. Because you have academics that way. And that learning has seeped into your temperament. Whatever we do physically now we need to do the same thing expressively.

## DELIGHT AVOIDS THIS ENTITY TO BE EFFICACIOUS IN LIFE

The one entity I have learned over the years is we are all so diverse. Our lives are so diverse. Our status quo is so different. Our experiences are so different. Our upbringings are so diverse. The journey of our life up until now for separately one of us is so different compared to somebody else DO NOT COMPARE yours or someone else's life with others.

ILLUSTRATION: If mister A can cover a distance of10 km in 1 hour. Where mister bed covers a distance of 10kms in 1.5 hours which one would you call faster and healthy? The answer would be mister a. now what if tell you that mister a prepared track to run on and mister b did by walking to the sanding path. I think our answer will now transformation we will undoubtedly think that mister be is fitter. Let's say principally mister a is 75 years old and mister b is only 20 here we go. Our answer changes again now we will think that 75 years ago is much healthier. Guess what?

Mister A weighs 60 kgs and mister B 125 kgs which makes it hard to run. What do you think now? Oh my god!! Now again we will correct our answer. The more we get to know about the strengths and limitations of mister A and B respectively. Our opinions and judgments about who's better, keep changing. And isn't life like that as well readers? We form opinions about others so quickly without knowing much about them and their situations. Judging people, labelling people. Life is not the same for all.

Some may not be as talented as others but make it better opportunities in the scale very fast. Whereas others dispute being super talented keep struggling just to make the ends meet. don't they say? That luck rules in palaces and at times talent keeps struggling on the streets? Some may have more resources while others lack them. Each one has different problems and so no solution can work for all. Just like one size of clothing doesn't fit all. So don't judge others" journey without knowing more. Don't judge your own life by looking at someone else's or comparing your situation with someone else's. you are you and they are they. Your life is your life, and their life is theirs. do take encouragement from others' expedition to enrich our own. And always reminisce. Life is the most problematic assessment many people fail because they try to copy others. Please realize that in life's exam Everyone has a diverse question paper.

# CHAPTER 3

# INDUSTRIOUS LIFE IS ALWAYS A SUSTAINING LIFE

So the first step is to wake up early at 5 am.

If you want to be efficacious in every way substantially, psychologically, ardently, and in your career.

Do yourself a favour, please wake up early and give yourself those early morning hours. If you study the lives of successful people, you will notice that they are early risers. Trust me you will be a better organizer. How? Envision yourself vertically in the topmost of the elevation efforts you will have assistance to perceive the unabridged city. Correspondingly, by arousing up early you can appear at your entire day and life and stratagem improved. Early risers are more active because they have time to comprehend the complications and contemplate resolutions and exertion upon them in a better way. So, let's have a conversation about the enchanted ness of these two early morning hours 5 am to 7 am. During the day the foremost constancy from our brain is the beta whitecaps. But in the morning, we unsurprisingly go into the alpha state, or we could even go into the theta state. So, at that time your mind is a dynamo of ingenuity. That's why her novelists, lyricists, and theorists rise early in the morning and love to exploit that golden time. And during the day there are so many disruptions to indistinct your mind. Envisage sitting at the airport and studying. We can do it but you will not be the greatest efficient at that time. In the morning the atmosphere is secluded. your mind is engrossed. You have just gotten up. It is hollow. So, for the learners, these two hours are unequivocally superlative. And the erudition you do throughout that time is identical to eight normal hours. Now let's talk about why people make it problematic to backwash up early? The reason is they have disrupted the rhythm of their body. There is an intrinsic bio clock that proposes laterally with the sun. Envisaged a hundred and fifty years ago there was no electricity in people's homes. So, after the sunset, there was not so much to do. So, people slept early, and naturally, they woke up early. But now fast forward by 150 years and what do we have? The homes are fully lighted, and people are on their campaigns till late at night. So naturally if you sleep late you are going to wake up late. How can you correct this? Between 10 and 11 at night the brain secrets a sleep-inducing chemical called melatonin if you can take advantage of that, you go off to sleep early, and when you do it day after day after day, the elimination of melatonin will increase making it easier for you to sleep at that time. But the superiority of sleep is also imperative. That is why two hours previously your bedtime put away all the electronics let the brain now start letting everything go itself and coming to a state where it can go to deep sleep. The quality of sleep is imperative if you wish to claim the morning. And before you sleep sit down for a few minutes scrutinize; these were the themes I needed to exert upon today. How far have I improved? make yourself meditative and then go to bed. In the morning when you wake up, you will be inspired. Now be very careful to protect that morning. Unfortunately, the first thing someone does when waking up is pulling the mobile and see what's the latest message on WhatsApp and any other social media. It's like fetching an extravaganza into your mind. That is why shields solo. Can you imagine a sadhu waking up after 6 in the morning? Why is it that saints that consecrated people today and always in antiquity have been awakening up early? These two fairylike hours when the atmosphere is tranquil, the atmosphere is peaceful, your mind is focused and undistracted and your brain is working at the alpha level. If you are a late riser, you cannot suddenly change things around. Start chipping away 15 minutes early, again. When you bring it to a desirable morning time, then you sustain it. It may be a little difficult initially but slowly it will work.

Miss world once said: Mediocrity is successful to reminisce what robe you show off, what kind of greasepaint you did, what your trinkets were like, whether your nails were highlighted or not. But they will reminisce about how you preserved them. And that is the foremost experience in life expectancy. That's the birth right dispensation in arrears.

## IF YOU WILL DO THIS TRUST ME IT WILL BE THE BEST DAYS OF YOUR LIFE.

It's not only about awakening up prematurely, it's approximately utilizing that precise stretch whereas awakening up early.

That period ought to be your furthermost industrious period.

So, let's start at 5 am. Wake up and sensation yourself. enthusiasm for open-air devours around renewed air.

Twitch with sequestered entreaty: Not all sequestered entreaty is effective, but the secluded devotions are always salaried. This is the diurnal the aristocrat has made. I will enjoy this day. Appreciations to go that you are tranquil flourishing there are thousands of origins to perish tranquil you are flourishing.

Trust me you will feel good with this early morning isolated entreaty. It can be of 5/10/15/20/30 minutes till what stretch you are enthusiastic in that entreaty.

Then nourish your concentration with a virtuous diet. And that diet is contemplation. Now you must be intelligent. Does it do anything? It all starts in the brain! During meditation, brain scans see augmented turmoil in provinces unswervingly interrelated with diminished nervousness and misery, lengthwise with augmented discomfort and lenience. The evasion approach grid, in precise, is galvanized when one's mind is relaxed and not converging on the exterior of the ecosphere, and has been originated to expand recollection, self-awareness, and goal scenery. Want to be additional caring to your friends and family? When scientists associated the bits of intelligence of Buddhist abbots with new meditators, they found the province of the intelligence accompanying the responsiveness to be much more obvious in the monks. It also accurately vicissitudes your intellect whitecaps- and we can quantify these occurrences. Meditators have higher levels of Leading Waves which have been shown to condense spirits of adverse disposition, arduousness, misery, and antagonism. And if that wasn't plentiful, it also substantially vicissitudes our brain shape and size. Think of your accomplishment as gruesome? In a study where both intermediaries and non-mediators were given a flu virus. meditators were able to produce a greater number of antibodies.

Now subsequently entreaty and contemplation you will sensation your intellect much ignitor. Lighter from anxiety, apprehension, and many more adverse feelings. Smiles will inexorably be on your face for a whole day. You will not get crabby or flashy to anyone.

So, after inspection, an unfilled gastrointestinal does something for your physique.

It can be a stride, yoga, consecutively, pedalling, or any other isometrics.

It's not that you are not substantially fit even if you are fat or something. It's because you have to be physically fit in the future also for your 50's to 90's.

Now you can start your diurnal tedious with school/college/office or anything.

Believe me, with this agenda you will be the thrilled and hassle-free unabridged day with exhausting a beautiful smile.

Then now let's talk about how you should end your day.

Snooze like a sovereign because you have accomplished your day bestowing to your plan thanks to God's former sleep. And take a cavernous sniffle and all antagonisms on or after this day it can be from any anthropological, state of affairs or entity will not come with you on next day. Yes, it ought to go with that day only for the reason that there is no practice of hauling that thing to an alternative day. Let's talk about this reason. If you sleep with some antipathies next morning you will think therefore you cannot think renewed with your old antipathies.


## PRACTICE THIS THING REGULARLY YOU WILL BE HABITUAL

Try this agenda at least 5 or 6 days a week and consider one as your cheat day.

Trust me none will be that satisfied from there as you are.

Before you die do bumpily that after your bereavement everyone could remember you.

So, for your industrious natural life one more thing you have to take pleasure from your life.

NEGATIVITY

Don't let undesirable people stop your vigour!

Adverse people are delinquent for every resolution. You should perimeter your stretch for the people who through your vigour.

## WHAT IS THE DESTINY YOU WANT FOR YOURSELF?

Let's say destiny for the next one year? What do you want? Gladness!! Yahoo!! These days few individuals say that life is a wave co-star. Do you say? What is the denotation of life as a wave coaster? What is the wave coaster? Where is the wave coaster? If someone is pleased with your home. We people say don't be happier because people are even frightened of being happier. If we will be happier, a bright eye can catch our contentment. Who has the malevolent appreciation?? How can it be imaginable?

For assistance: you are apart, and ABC is identical content wearing an attractive costume and you are sensitively resentful of her and throughout the gathering, you are blaspheming her gratified descent, please fall why? Because you can't see her glad and gorgeous. Do you think she will fall??? Some readers will think yes because it may give you evil eyes. But I think now she will not fall. because the girl with a beautiful dress is not thinking the same. Now all of us are creating thoughts trying to send a vibration that now falls please fall we are those who are sending negative quivering. Now, will she fall??? No. So how do we humans say evil eyes can catch you?

This is what has to be taken care of. Your karma is creating your destiny and what is your karma? Your thoughts yes, your thoughts. Instead, everyone is praying that she should fall if she only is thinking that I shall fall then only she will.

Life goes like this:

Opinions

Frame of mind

Arrogance

Accomplishment

Convention

Temperament

Vocation


So, start fashioning wrong opinions destiny has started getting distressed. Start creating the right thoughts and destiny will change.

There are two ways to life live

1. Wanting to know what we inscribed in my destiny.

2. Create a destiny I want.


Early in the morning, we used to read the newspaper's zodiac signs.

There it may be written 'cautious today someone will swindler you' What is the foundation of my supposed? STATISTICS. And today I will see everyone with misgiving's eyes.

For example, I am in my office inspecting my subordinate and senior talk with others. Maybe they are only duplicitous to me. For 4 days I am inspecting them both to talk about something clandestinely.

Now, what's the destiny I have formed for that day? Then come home and say that the horoscope from this newspaper is 100% true. I will read this recurrently. Because what had been inscribed on my zodiac sign exactly happened to me.

Suppose it was nonsense like that I hadn't read that newspaper until somebody cheated on me then? Then what? I would not generate erroneous opinions throughout the day so I will be passionately sturdy and if somebody tricks me just cross it and face it with pride. Just think 'it's okay if any of the 100 people we come across will do something someday. On the other hand, if I read that zodiac insignia, I will generate nervousness. I will hesitate, and then that one person who pretended to cheat me when he cheats me. I don't have the forte to face that state I previously misplaced. And now this horoscope was only one day something they tell for a year, maybe for five years, and maybe more than that. Now what we will do is? We will exert but there will continuously be an allegation inside us. I will do this, but this precise entity won't be efficacious because my horoscope said this at least for 5 years.

Your brain: is alienated into two halves. Optimistic and adverse. virtuous and malicious. It doesn't function on an experimental nonentity. Constructive and adverse. Decent and malevolent. It doesn't function on nonentity. Aren't any nonaligned ground in your brain. It's either optimistic or decent, or undesirable or malicious. You are the one who will designate it.

So, all your prerequisite to organize is. Just be the technique your famine to be. How famished are you? That's all. It's that unassuming but also that distant away, isn't it? It's that unpretentious; Afterall your neediness to be ecstatic; just be the way who is discontinuing you? No, no they are responsible for this. See, now:

You don't crave to do what they poverty to do. But you crave to do what you starve to do. This is untruly. If you're craved, do what you want to do. You must also be okay with everybody doing what they want to do. This is the only way because self-determination is a two-way watercourse, isn't it? Yes? Now if somebody is substantially excruciating you? If that is so, you come; we will take you away because then you need to be endangered. Nonentity is substantially agonizing you; they are just responsible for what they want to do, they are saying what they want to say. Or they're just axioms that distinguish them, aren't they? So, who is triggering the mess within you? Yourself. Because somewhere you believe, if you become annoyed, if you convert downhearted, it may pay off.

And it does occasionally. If there are more despondent societies around you who are worth your anguish. It pays off, isn't it? Yes? If you act miserable in the house. you get many things; if you are joyful or maybe you don't get it. Right? So, you learn the trick so what you need to comprehend is artificial is double fringed. If you are miserable, whatever the hell you get, it doesn't mean whatsoever. If you are thrilled, you didn't get whatever so who is esophagi.., this is not just artificial. Everybody around us has constantly been playing this pretence and you supposed that's the way; but what is it that you crave is? Do we want to be ecstatic or dejected? So, just be the technique you want to be. Does it invade anybody? Now, I want to participate, if I do, now this is successful to base some quarrel on somebody. I just want to be happy. Is it surpassing anybody's anything? I am asking? So, you are the way you want to be, who is suspending you? You cannot do whatever your craving does, but you can be the way your craving unites to be, isn't it? yes? Can anybody break you? Others need not even know that you are ecstatic if they are like a despondent appearance, elasticity to them. If they have identical despondent appearances, stretch it to them, but you can still be joyful, right? Right now, we will experiment, okay?

Right now, a lot of appearances are observing ecstatic. I want you to preserve the equivalent pleasure and look despondent. Do it now, do it now, let me see; don't grin. Show me your despondent expression; existence ecstatic within you. You must rehearse. Look this will be desirable in your home. If you spend all the time hahaha they'll go senseless. Occasionally, they suppose a despondent expression. What's so mystical about you, all this damn yoga hehe and all? What's the problem? Accomplishment ought to be the way the condition stresses; have I not been insistent on this all the time? But you tell me which is chief, your way of animation is foremost, r accomplishment is original? Which originates foremost? Your way of presence! So, if you say I want to be ecstatic, begin that. Accomplishment, as the state of affairs anxieties. Approximately civilization likes unhappiness, some people like amusement, some people deplorable do it. Please repeat life with meditation as I told you previously. Happenstance with veracity, you know it ought to materialize now not subsequently when you are concluding this book. What I am expressive of you is, the whole thing you do is, in fact, an act. Isn't that so? Moreover, you do it determinedly or you do it extemporaneously. If you do it mechanically, you think it's real, and actually, it's an act. isn't it so? The whole lot is roasted up in your skull isn't it, whatever you do? So, it's nonetheless a performance. So, do you want to do it determinedly or do you want to do it spontaneously? That's all the major is.

So, you do it instinctively and you think it's real, it's the foolish way to exist. It's any way an act; at least do it intentionally, then life will be stunning. If you do it instinctively its attendance is equivalent to a trick. It's not trickery. Life is not deception because the evacuation is continuously here, wide open. Yes, or no? So, if the exodus was anchored, only then you can call it a trick, isn't it. The material is constantly open one instant if you don't take care, you'll be dead. Your whole life is to somehow not influence the exit. Isn't it so? So, it is not a trap, it is just that, if you contemplate that your entertainments are all factual, then its ambiances are like a trap. Whatever you think. feel or do is your act. isn't it? When you do not realize it's your act, you think it is God-given command. You will start to reach the ability to speak. When you hear voices, it's very clear you need comportment. So, you want to know the uppermost state of pleasantness, isn't it? So, who is discontinuing you no, but they're doing this? Do whatever you want to do if you instigate your way of being hen whatsoever you do it's just an interrogation on the state of affairs contingent on what kind of status quo exists.

## ACTION IS AS THE SITUATION DEMANDS AND OFFERS. ISN'T IT?

Let me give you an example: "No I want to be my own thing, there is no your own thing", "No I want to become IT proficient." There is no such damn entity. Because you are born in India, you are thinking of IT proficiency. Suppose you were born here years ago and you're thinking of fishing in the ocean, isn't it?

When complications are beyond our control.

In the former 100 or 150 years through the formulation of science and technology, we have added luxuries and expediencies than any peers that could ever envisage. We are the furthermost relaxed peers ever substantially, immensely, nonetheless, can we say we are the most pacific peers, ecstatic, affectionate. No!!

Or we can uniform around we are furthermost intellectual peers? That will be the erroneous entity to approximately. Any bibliophile prerogative that he/she is intellectual expands to imprudence, isn't it? For the reason that the consequence of cleverness is it demonstrates to you how many ambiguities there are in your astuteness. Only clown belongings there are no ambiguities accurately intellectual creatures continuously about is how numerous ambiguities in my astuteness. This is approximately what your indispensability does to yourself when you are fledgling. It doesn't matter what you want to do in your life, one entity must emerge from your physique and your acumen should not be instigated in your way. They are an inevitable exertion for you. Your physique and your concentration ought never to derive in your mode who you crave to be. Precise now for furthermost individual, they are an immense matter when you have a matter how will you elevate matters in the world? If you categorically want to discourse on matters in the world this one should not ever be a matter. Understood? I have not the matter here, I have not ever the trick. If there are snags I will pact through it. But I am at no time tricky. This must materialize to you, doesn't it? Make yourself like this.

YOU ARE NEVER THE PROBLEM YOU ARE ALWAYS THE PART OF SOLUTION never the part of the tricky. Precisely now we have industrialized an arrogance in a nation all are the persons for each explanation they invent trickily. So, there are people who are too tricky. There is the public who is occupied with explanations. Undeveloped individuals ought to attitude awake and develop an explanation for forthcoming peers to derive in your own life to bloom. Since the extreme fulfillment in life is that your role in such a way you can do approximately that is much greater than yourself. This must materialize. This is the highest accomplishment of commotion.

TO DO SOMETHING LARGER THAN YOURSELF only then your willpower sees the implementation in the commotion. Commotion is one entity. But the utmost imperative entity is how you stand? when you are unaided. It might seem despondent that you are in an immoral corporation, isn't it? (unserious) all the young people ought to do this to yourself at least with three days you ought to be seated unaccompanied no television, no texting no nothing let's perceive what happens you necessity identify the nature of who you are, you essential distrustful yourself one day you will be discovered into almost you must know what is the level of psychosis you are anguish when I say psychosis if your concentration is out of your resistor is it called psychosis in delimitation? Just see what all your concentration does. You resolve don't tell anyone you only resolve the level of psychosis you are profitable concluded. If you arrive in this ecosphere, what will you produce? You will solitary generate who you are, isn't it? What you are is what will happen to the world about you. Beforehand you stage out in the world is it not imperative at least you're this much apparatus that you are not problematic.

## DISPENSATION THIS ONE ENTITY FOR YOUR SELF-WORTH

Don't try to renounce since what will you renounce? What is it that you are working to renounce? If you curve miserable, that is not renunciation. That's virtuous isometrics. If you acknowledge I have capitulated. That's atrocious self-worth. So, how will you renounce what you will renounce? What have you become to renunciation first of all? It is out of a convinced consciousness. the renunciation happens. It's when you perceive that these confrontations are very can be very ambiguous because you have continuously been imparted, self-worth, self-esteem, assurance, isn't it? These are the treasured possessions to variety your life. Renunciation is in contradiction of all these belongings. Only when you are valueless can you renounce, please see. If you have self-worth, self-esteem, assurance. How to renounce? But can you breathe without assurance; can you live without self-esteem or some sense of self-worth? Right now, no? see, I have no sagacity of self-esteem or self-worth that's why any instant I am enthusiastic to go. Since I think this is wealth whatsoever. In my view, I don't contemplate this value whatsoever. Keeping this on but for the reason that it appears to be convenient for various survivors around us, we preserve this success. But there is no self-worth. For the intellect of self, the situation is departed, so anywhere is the cost. Density is not worth whatsoever and that which is not worth anything. If you add reverence, that's masses of anxiety. And as of this reverence, this insignificant thing if it converts self-assured, that's factual anxiety, but for that the greater good of endurance for people whispered, people only whispered, it's not accurate. People whispered except. You have faith in yourself, you cannot endure. It's not factual. It's not accurate in an indispensable way. If people whispered that and it developed a factual procedure for them. Because whatsoever you have faith in if you complement adequate focus and sentiment upper it, it converts factual. Do you recognize? It develops very factually. All varieties of ridiculous credence structures around the creation have developed categorically factual for masses of persons. Not for an insignificant quantity of people. For an enormous mainstream of the populace, it's converted factually. They have faith in it, and it is so. as of credence these possessions have converted factually. But whatsoever you have faith in and whatsoever you authorize with your opinions and your sentiments., has no experiential foundation. When you talk capitulation, you are talking to a nearby transitory. Transitory from restrictions of one measurement to an alternative. You collided your skull on the wall satisfactorily, that now you comprehend that except you developed comparable reedy mid-air, you will not be authorized. When you have realized this, in your contemporary procedure you will never authorize, when you grasp this. Example: you are restrained, and the accesses are impenetrable, and nonentity transpires, you can't enthusiasm.

There is a drain, grimy drain. If you conclude this obscenity, you can get out of self-determination. Will you indicate that crawling concluded the obscenity or not? you will, right? Yes? If that's the direction to liberty/ to the most horrifying filth, you will be crawling. It will go into your nostrils and your aperture ubiquitously, but it doesn't matter, it's chief to your liberty. You will crawl to conclude obscenity. That's surrender. That's surrender because you have comprehended you can't annoy the residential walls vertically that is why you are Rawling. So, capitulation is a convinced understanding that you comprehend in your contemporary procedure. You cannot authorize the entrance. So, your novelty is an additional intellectual technique to authorization. That determination does not come by agronomy, that will derive only by a confident comprehension; moreover, out of your brainy or for the reason that life has pulverized you appropriately or that you're impractical abundant to fall in love with an unrestrained way, not in a provisional way, not in a serviceable way, not in a pleasant technique, in an impractical way. Impractical like a Ramakrishnan or a marabi or Akka mahadevi. There have been many numbers; these are the acknowledged designations. There have been a number of them. Who is impractical? They are not well-balanced, they are not agreeable, not at all enjoyable, I want you to know but they are eccentric and that which is eccentric need not be nice. Usually, it's not nice. NEVER GIVE UP.


## CONCENTRATION

When a person sits on the vertebral bench of the car as a nearside, he has an excellent ability to do numerous things. He can talk on the phone, can see here and there, can talk with the person seated next to him, annoy, beverage, perceive the cars or the announcements external. But the motorist cannot see here and there, cannot see the memorandum. Why? Because if the driver gets unfocussed then significance could be a coincidence. The expedition of life as well, if we get distracted, we cannot ever achieve what we want. And if we want to circumvent getting unfocussed. We have to start in concert with the protagonist, a motorist. As long as we play the role of curb side, we remain preoccupied. We will endure preoccupied ness in our associations, in our exertion and our everyday responsibilities, in our otherworldly life, in our particular life, and our psychological steadiness. If we want to accomplish something in life and influence our terminology, we will have to portray the protagonist of a motorist in our life. We have to jump captivating custody of our voyage. We keep our phones but disremember to custody our subsists, we responsibility our processors but disremember to take custody of the expedition of our life. If you want to be gradually interchanged in your life, absorb to take custody. Stop in concert the protagonist of curb side, stop peaceful. Accept the protagonist of the motorist. BE FOCUSED with one-pointed devotion and you twitch liability this, you will accomplish accomplishment in what you do.

## KNOW HOW TREASURED YOU ARE

A man once called his son and told him that he would give him to some degree astonishing, approximately tremendously appreciated. He dragged out a red velvety container and moderately unfastened it. Privileged the container was an old wristwatch. As he tendered the wristwatch over his son, the man said: "This watch is very superior". It has become miserable to us over 3 cohorts and is at least over 200 years old. You can practice it. You can retain it as a chronicle or impartial peddle it and get currency to acquire whatsoever you like" a diminutive disenchanted, the young son looked at his father and said, "dad, this is so outmoded. I don't think I can wear it. And it is so old, I am not uniform sure if it possibly will be peddled." The man took his son to a horologist shop nearby to show him how valuable the watch was. The watchmaker scrutinized the timepiece judiciously and said, "Since the watch is so old, all I can give you for this is 5 dollars. The young man turned to his father with an expression on his face which was like "I told you right? "The father then took his son to a hostage shop where they offered him a loan for personal items kept in security. The owner of the pawnshop looked at the watch for a while, turned to the man, and said. "You expect coinage for this quantity of scuffle? All we would do with this is we would have it in the bunkum bin. Sorry, we cannot offer anything for this" unremitting, the man now took his son to a museum. They went to see the foremost of the museum, who was proficient in the worth of old things. When the chief saw the watch, he exclaimed. "Incredible, so well manufactured! Such meticulousness in its innovativeness! Look at the eminence of the constituents. A watch like this is priceless. But we can offer you a million dollars for this. Thank you for indicating to come to us with this watch, they said. The young man stood their God smacked with eyes wide open not even intermittent, as his father, the gratified proprietor of the watch, very, fortunately, accepted the transaction. And sold the historic quantity for a million dollars. As they both sauntered vertebral home, the ancestor said: always know this one thing son. Like the watch, you will only be valued if you are in a precise dwelling. Horologists' restoration watches. Their eyes can see tiny attachments and watch fragments. But an erroneous residence for a historic portion like this. Pawn workshops use them as collateral, they can only see everything based on their current market value. Wrong place for a historic quantity like this. But at a museum that displays antique, valuable, antiques, connoisseurs can see beyond watch parts, beyond the current market charges of watches. They can see the authentic value of the entity. Unquestionably the precise apartment for a historic portion like this. If you find yourself not esteemed, don't get fuming or unfulfilled! Know that you are undoubtedly in an erroneous apartment being arbitrated by people who see minuscule fragments of you, minuscule fragments of your life, not the unabridged you. Or being justice of the peace to people who see you for how copious your net wealth is. How much is your contemporary market value? They see you for what you have, not for what you are. Appearance for those who can see your real worth somewhere else all externals who have the proficient visualization to see the accurate you yonder all your deficiencies and all your culpabilities. Those who can see your true worth, your factual budding, will stimulate you to do well, to live well, to love, to grow, and to rise in life. EVERY INDIVIDUAL HAS A SPECIAL SENSE OF WORTH. All we need is someone who can see that worth in us and make us see that worth in ourselves as well. YOU ARE VALUABLE

## YOU'RE AN ORIGINAL

A plum once said "on my dear lord" can you gratify make me a banana? Did God say why? Since that guy loves bananas. So, God said, "so be it" the plum converted a banana. So then the guy came. As a substitute, he procured an orange. The plum turns out to be a banana for the same guy and the guy procures an orange. The banana said, "please give me an orange". God said "so be it" become an orange., So that guy selected the orange bit and spat it saying it's acrimonious. That orange said- my dead lord, can you please make me Graper? God, please said- so be it. Orange became Graper and the guy didn't unfluctuating look at the grapes. And the grapes said "how I wish I persisted with a plum. There would be someone who could originate and yield to me. Dear readers, we all are diverse. God has created each one of us to be diverse. Our landscapes are diverse. Our guises are diverse. Ours adores and dislikes are all diverse. The whole world is specific. Everybody is diverse. All are dissimilar. Why do you want to be like somebody else? Why do you famine to be like the big shot else? Why are you an impertinent god? He twisted you. Why are you rude to him- that you didn't tell me precisely. That is why I want to be like him/her. Booklovers, how many of you don't like mangoes? Just because someone likes mango should a plum become a mango? Just because someone likes plums, should a mango become a plum? If you are plum please remain a plum. If you are a mango, please remain a mango. You are twisted to be corresponding to this. Be glad, be yourself. Realize who you are. Don't review individuals. Follow your appetite. Trail your nature. Discover who you are! Finding out where you fit, not just being a member of Hurd hurtling the herd. Dear readers, you are innovative. WHY DO YOU WANT TO BE A PHOTOCOPY OF OTHERS? Inventiveness is worth it. I want to sing like him/her… why?? I want to dance like him?? Why??? If you don't know how to dance just sing!! As simple as that. If you don't know how to sing, just study, or speak or whatsoever just be inventive. It is always there that you can do. YOU ARE YOU. Why should I make a damned fool by doing what somebody else is doing? That's not my forte. That's his or her forte. You categorize what is your strong point. You all are diverse. Each one is diverse. Don't vary this damn error of wearisome to be like somebody else. The chief error you can make in your 20's is to try and track somebody and be them. You can take encouragement from them. But you can't rival them.

## THIS APPELLATION WILL ASSISTANCE YOU GET CONSTANT IN LIFE

Cantankerousness is an indicator of an out-equilibrium life. Constancy in our retorts is an indication of life in equilibrium. We are cantankerous, we snap, we retort at the drop of a bonnet for minutiae. Unbiased as you are out of balance. People who have sensible life know how to holder gravity. People whose subsists are not well-adjusted basin under compression and grow so cantankerous at diminutive belongings. And they unbiased kind of instant off, you know. And consequently, I undeniably feel all of us have to learn to be from the Mahabharata this character called YUDHISTHIR. the very name Yudhishthira in Sanskrit yudhi + sthira = stable in chaos (battle). Dear book lovers, we can't stop pandemonium in our lives, can we? Life is not gonna be ideal. There is always going to be some exhaust that will need extra devotion than the other. Every so often your strength requests more devotion, from time to time your spouse needs more consideration., occasionally your exertion desires additional kindness, and yet from time to time your friends need more devotion. It's continuously doing to variation. Life is very dynamic. It's not one kind of sturdy graph that's okay. wife all through my life. I give time to my wife or work. Some people are like that, overachievers. Some people are like that, Wilkins. Sorry if I devised that axiom you know. It's continuously going to be an identical energetic entity. Diverse characteristics will prerequisite urgencies at dissimilar epochs in life.


## FIND THE FINE EQUILIBRIUM IN CONSTRUCTING YOUR VICTORY

As I came to one of the science laboratories. I saw a pendulum in full momentum., swinging from one end to another and I was persuaded that eventually, it would come to a standstill, accurate in the center deprived of animation on moreover of the immoderations. It ought to myself so much in our life be contingent on being centered and not inclining in the direction of dangerous divergences. Over the years, I've met people who have accomplished enormous accomplishments in what they do. But they recognize their accomplishment due to their imaginative nature. To their energies and their endeavours. They believe it's their husting unaccompanied that has transported them to anywhere they are currently. You can occasionally fragrance an intelligence of superiority in their arrogance and thorn. After all, in this unfair world, they have impressed a place for themselves, the self-made ones. One danger of the plumb: the self-made self-starters. And I also met those who praise pardon. They are too precise people. To the correct masteries. To the right environs. To the golden breaks that came their way, maybe to karma, luck, or destiny. And some even to higher powers of God. These personalities are truthful in accepting that there are people and forces beyond themselves, responsible for their accomplishment. Most often they come diagonally as retiring but they trust that their exertion had no protagonist in their accomplishment. These are the sanctified ones. Other extremes of the pendulum. THE BLESSED DEFENDERS. Conclusion success in what we do is such an implausible equilibrium. As human beings we have an unrestricted will, we have unconventionality. We can indicate. And undeniably it is the proper use of that free will. And indeed, it is the appropriate use of that free will. DIRECTING OUR RESOURCES, ENERGY, AND POWER IN THE RIGHT PLACE BRINGS SUCCESS. And that accomplishment, that achievement brings self-confidence and belief in our unlimited potential, but we cannot deny the fact that our independent efforts reach a limit and unless help comes from outside. It's hard or unfluctuating and intolerable to transfer to the next level. It is at that time; we start realizing our triviality, we start realizing our reliance on rudiments outside of ourselves.

Self-confidence transmogrified into unpretentiousness and those who continuously whispered that they are dependant need to balance their modesty, self-esteem After All the car may be pre-arranged to you, the road map can also be given to you but unless you drive the care, you don't reach your terminus. So, isn't it imperative that we also feel well-intentioned and virtuous about ourselves by eloquent words that we have an imperative fragment to produce in this voyage of accomplishment as well? Dear readers, I was augmented by what the plumb imparted to me. Accomplishment is the equilibrium amongst our self-determining exertions and dependence on others. It is the amalgamation of credence in our immeasurable worth and knowledge of our inconsequentiality. Eloquent that I have margins that only be equipoise with the kind assistance of others it is a well-balanced tactic that makes accomplishment factual, and nourishing SUCCEED WITH SATISFACTION

## CLANDESTINE IN ARREARS THE PRECEDING CONFRONTATIONS OF THE DYING MAN

And a mature man was on his bereavement bed, capitulating by his intimate. As he was about to exhale his former, hardly able to voice, he sympathetically underway inarticulate. Lemon. Everybody around him was unequivocally disorganized. What did he mean? Was he asking for lemons? And even if he was asking for lemons, what would he do with lemons now?? As all of them were trying to make some sense. Out of what was happening, the man passed away. The family members performed his final rites and to honour his last words even gave loads of lemons in charity. A couple of months later all the family members came together and mutually agreed to sell the house and the property that the dead man left behind to a builder. The builder to whom the property was sold, pulled the house down with a desire to build a high-rise building on those same possessions. One day as his men were digging under the ground, they found an enormous treasure chest with huge amounts of gold, diamonds, and precious gems and jewels. One of the neighbours who was living in the neighbourhood took a memo of this and intimated the family of the dead man. When the family came to encounter the constructor to claim the paragon trunk that was instituted in their old possessions, the producer underprivileged philanthropic them the paragon torso, saying that once the property was purchased, whatever came along with the possessions was his. The intimate event took the constructor to the law court, but the court reigned in the favour of the constructor. One day swiftly the grandson of the dead man-made construction. At the very spot under which the paragon torso was initiated in the square used to happen to be the lemon tree, oh my god!! Was that what grandpa was trying to interconnect when he was an incoherent lemon? Right under that lemon tree was concealed a paragon chest. The family adherents had walked around in the courtyard numerous times. The grandson had occupied himself with cricket right under the lemon tree several times. And all of them had missed the treasure veiled right beneath the ground that they were walking on. What a shame!! There is a treasure hidden deep within every single one of us. We are all gifted with something very distinct, something very unique, deep within us, out of the 7 billion people living on the planet earth, none can be YOU. You do not try to be somebody else. Be yourself. Dig deep within yourself. Dig out the grime of contentment. Dig out and pull out the dirt of self-doubt, dig out the dirt of conformism of social standards of success. And discover that treasure deep within you was gifted and blessed with. And when that self-discovery happens, not only will you be super effective, but you will find deep satisfaction within the core of your heart. The next time you see lemons remember that you have to BEGIN THE JOURNEY OF SELF-DISCOVERY. Even if it is late and to be honest it is never too late.

When I was in school one of my friends lent my notebook to a vicious circle with some of the programs he had untapped and not to my associate copied one of the dissertations that I had written. He then used it for an essay rivalry. Which he concluded up by captivating. When I got to know I felt embittered. I was very distraught and felt that this was absolute burglary. Another time a Ph.D. student told me that her instructor took her research paper and published it in his name. People working in the corporate world have told me that they found reports that were strenuously stolen by their contemporaries for their gain. Novelists have often complained of plagiarism as well. And surely whichever work area it is, maybe we should deal with people who have such a dishonest, distorted mindset. At the same time, we should also remember that what we possess is way beyond an essay. Way beyond a research paper or a report. A bird once asked a honeybee; you work so hard; you toil so much. You put so much effort and energy to make and store honey. And then a man comes and steals it. Do you not feel sad? The honeybee gave a fantastic reply. Yes, I felt sad at that moment. But then I remind myself that the only thing a man can steal from me is "honey". He can never steal my art of making honey that he possesses again. We certainly need to deal with such cheating practically and we also need to be aware that people can at best copy our creation, not our creativity. They can at best steal our techniques, not our talent. They can imitate what we do but cannot take away our ability to inspire. This is why I say focus on and grow that which none can steal. And let everything else. Simply be a manifest result of it

## TEN CAUSE WHYS AND WHEREFORES QUIET INDIVIDUALS ARE EFFICACIOUS

Have you ever conjectured why quiet individuals are efficacious?

One of the psychology theories that split humans into two categories of temperament is constructed on how they get vigour.

One who becomes their vigour from existence on the external and socialization is called gregarious, while one who becomes their vigour from unaccompanied while is called a reclusive. How do self-confidence and introspection correlate with accomplishment? Some of the abilities of a successful person are often allied with a vociferous person, exclusively in a field that necessitates supplementary community speaking and schmoozing. However, some of the most efficacious and persuasive people in the world are homebodies. There are a bunch of efficacious silent people such as Bill Gates, Mark Zuckerberg, and Albert Einstein. Here are the reasons why quiet people are successful.

**1.** They are prodigious proposers. Silent people often need more time to progress evidence in their craniums. That is the reason why they do not converse much. With the capability to deliberate things concluded, it makes them great proposers.

They would come up with numerous circumstances in their heads for the reason that they don't see the purpose why a creature should talk much except if it is obligatory. To prosper in any pitch, one requirement generates campaigns and accomplishes them. This necessitates a lot of intellect, and it would not be done by conversation only.

**2.** They are good auditors: quiet people are successful without a crosscut. A person will not instantaneously become successful; it will take a lot of advice and improvement to finally succeed on the quest. To be able to accept advice well, one requirement is to be a good eavesdropper. This doesn't necessarily mean people who love to talk more are not good eavesdroppers. It is more because silent people often let others talk first, so they receive more feedback to help them succeed.

**3.** They are imaginative: silent people prefer to occupy a supplement of their time within their heads instead of talking to people. During their unaccompanied time, they often engender philosophies and relationship philosophies that resulted in creative work. Inventiveness is imperative to accomplish an occupation since clienteles often choose variability. The cause why some silent people are successful is that they use their inventiveness to produce and increase their occupation. This form of person usually will surprise their peers with unconventional or innovative ideas.

**4.** They indicate their confrontations judiciously: if you want to be efficacious but are anxious about people arbitrating you for being an inaudible creature, there is a great characteristic of people who choose stillness. A good correspondent is not restricted to individuals who like to converse. Quiet people tend to express less than others but once they do, it's arranged that they have evaluated their words judiciously. Indicating the precise confrontations and emphasizing the important message is more tactful to persuade a prospective commercial client. As a quiet person, you spend more time deciding what to say and what you do not say.

**5.** They are great spectators: a status quo where one person does the conversation and others just vacation in the background means it is likely for that letter to announce their surroundings more. In an occupation, it is imperative to perceive the targeted market by using cues. Silent people are successful since they are apt to their surroundings; they can see an outline and practice it for their subsequent supplementary. The presence of a good spectator also attends as an advantage if you work in a field that requires a lot of approaches.

**6.** They preserve only the best individuals: homebodies are likely more discriminatory in their social circle. They don't mind having only a few friends and confidants, but they know they can count on them. If you are an introvert, you prefer quality over extent. Therefore, notwithstanding being a moderate person, schmoozing is immobile conceivable. The transformation of networking between soundless and flashy ones is the affiliation is habitually premeditated. A reclusive entrepreneur knows who he should subordinate himself with. It helps to create both advantageous and meaningful relationships.

**7.** They know their significance: think there are not any good potential of silent people left? It's unbelievable how a characteristic that's often seen is a feebleness that has a proportion of optimistic margins. Silent people may not be the most fun at get-togethers, but they know their priorities.

Why some silent people are successful is that they know where they stand, and they stick to their beliefs. For example, a person who focuses on a food and beverage industry knows that this is their priority before expanding their business to an unrelated field. A consistent effort and the right priorities are more likely to result in success.

**8.** They can expand trust straightforwardly: whereas being a trusted person may not have something to do with how someone gets their liveliness, it is understandable that others think silent people are more trustworthy. Not having a conversation all the time is also a sign of good self-discipline. They know that some belongings are improved and left implicit. Specifically, if it deals with confidential material. Take a banker who undoubtedly knows the password of your savings book or an intelligence agent who knows an undisclosed secret. People choose them for their ability to zip their aperture and not spill enigmas all over the place.

**9.** They are self-conscious: another purpose, because silent people are successful, is they are aware of their capability and their inadequacies. They know that every start-up will not skyrocket in an instant. As a result, they are prospective to follow a sequencer to advance themselves and to fill the gap of their flaws with other qualities. Self-consciousness is not to be erroneous with being self-conscious. Being self-aware means they know they lack something, but instead of whining about it. They seek an explanation to make the best of their flaws.

**10.** They have good self-discipline: as specified previously, silent people tend to have good self-discipline. Existence, self-cognizance, and concentrating on a solitary entity means they don't overindulge themselves in stuff that will not assist them. With this superiority, some silent individuals are successful because they know what they should do and what they should not do. They focus on their productivity instead of pleasing people.

## CONCLUSION

Being quiet in a gaudy world can be threatening, but once quiet people know their worth, the world will transform with them. The key is to know and to exploit these potentials. Silent people have many qualities, as revealed above. That will support them to be efficacious. Their capabilities to think profoundly, to know when to state, and to observe are some reasons why silent people are more successful than they are supposed to be. Hopefully, by erudition the virtuous side of certainty is reclusive; it will assist the silent people out there to start making actual change and become successful.

# CHAPTER 4

# HOW TO CREATE YOUR HAPPINESS?

Being annoyed is informal or respond tranquillity is informal? Each booklover traverses automatically if approximately is in your cognizance that I said ABC to do this and he did this. In short, if possessions are not going conferring to you being annoyed is tranquil or respond calmly is easy? These days what happening is in that thing if we are at loss, we blame others easily. Humans these days think "now who will talk calmly, I know he will not agree" we choose to scold instead. And in real also work get done if we scold someone, he will do that particular work quickly. And we think this way is easily inconvenient. Now if we notice for 10-20 years, we get many works done. I had done an event last year we have done many arrangements, decoration, catering, invitations, etc., etc. All arrangements have been done in 10 days many humans were underwritten to this one thing I have appreciated in this arrangements task is not everyone did it successfully but there were many mistakes were done in between but none have shouted. None blamed any of them. Because God teaches us the situation our inside situation service can be done by their only. The arrangement has been done everything was flawless this is not service. Service is the condition of your mind while doing all this. Calm mind with pure ambiance. Now let's shift this situation to our office word. We all do hard work a lot of exertion. Even these days we don't have time to sit even. After this much rigid exertion also you are construing this chapter that how to be happy? But if we ask that why you do this much hard work everyone will say for our happiness. If we are doing hard work for our contentment only so why we are not attainment glad? Essentially, we were doing rigid work to receive very imperative money. Today without money we can do nonentity. We all have the accountability to gross Money, take care of our parents, spouses. We have to do and everything but in the intervening time we have to calm our mind this thing we all should rehearsal with that what things are you doing for your loved ones you can give contentment too otherwise our family got everything. Everyone is partaking a house, cars, phone there is nonentity we don't have. But contentment, prosperity, and delightful associations why they are traumatized? Because will be earning that money and everything we didn't care about our mental peace. So, the brain is extinguishing with that well-being subjects are insertion. 20 years before from 100, there were only 1 or 2 having cancer and other health problems. Now malignancy is so ordinary like typhoid. Unhappiness was a very immense substance but now 99% of booklovers may also have despair. Someone from a divorced family doesn't even tell anyone nowadays they nonchalantly say there was a sympathetic problem, so we called her home and remarried. See, this much assessment has been transformed so we are determined not to change all this another 10 years' comparison will approximately be. So, relationships, contentment, and prosperity will not come from hard work. Only handling will come from rigid exertion but not contentment. Extravagances can come from hard work but no pleasure. Rigid exertion will give you superficial armistice only but a not innermost armistice. So, is it conceivable to be happy all the time? Always? Is it imaginable? Yes, !! How? Let me tell you. if your brain's battery-operated is thrilling in an expectant way you and your intimate everyone will be happy all the time. But if that series is liquidated then we and others everyone will get bad-tempered. But we get annoyed our battery-operated gets sharpened. You have to learn that the whole lot cannot be bestowed to you constantly is there any intimate who got bestowing to you 100%?? Not even in your bureau meteorological conditions you are a supervisor. Our correspondence is if the public will go bestowing to me then I am happy otherwise not.

Now someone emanates an approximately solitary unity stroke and enthusiasm. have you, veteran, it? Someone emanated and alleged unbiased a stroke or perhaps unfluctuating an expression and go. After that how many appearances are approximately related to that stroke? We one after the other re-emergence that stroke in our cognizance and variety mug of that then our soul becomes hefty then we contemplate 'I prerequisite to segment this with someone. We say undesirable lines this much then we say that ABC offended us. They impartial whispered a stroke we solitary repetitive it 100 epochs and diverse that stroke with numerous further belongings. Then we call our friend or anyone and told him/her a page. Although a dispute amongst two souls. The vigour of the soul will diminution. An argument can be of 20 min/30min or an hour battery gets low because our soul is using negative energy in that (positive energy never gets battery discharge of your soul). After an argument, we usually don't talk for a while, one or two days but still, we are speaking to respectively supplementary although reversing that argument. With this, our soul's battery gets emancipation swiftly than an argument. That negative thoughts in our mind become peculiar troposphere in dynasty also.

Unfortunately, as grownups, whether your parents or not this is what our children are erudition from us. You see how demanding we are every day. They sense our anxiety and they timepiece our scuffle to find our contentment. So how do we go from apprehension and misery to happiness? Some virtuous news. The world contentment description also states that the best prognosticator of whether a child becomes a satisfied adult is through their emotional health in childhood.

There is research successful in Hayward for 75 years. This is the chief research so far. About modification amongst the life of anthropology, you live opportunely or miserable. They were exploring the modification amongst humans who live there pleasing and who live unsatisfied life.

Lastly, an opportunity was mortals with upright connotations sojourn delighted in their occurrences. Creatures through corrupt concerns, unsteady concerns live disgruntled. Howard was an enterprise reconnoitre of accurate anthropological afterward creatures of 16. Now few are doctors/ lawyers etc. You have proficient proportions, but affiliation is consecrated. What will you do with this life? Dispassionate cautious nearby it? We all categorize empathetic as most imperious, but we don't escalate anybody.

Instance: We distinguish how to plunge, we unbiased have to expand our needles and appendages.

Booklovers prompt me this even though fluttering indicators and forelegs contain rotation?

Analogous as we categorize, we precondition to escalate but can we understand in genuine? Can an attachment apply? With the axiom "empathetic should be around" Real learnedness resources real-world technique.

Almost everything is erroneous in our endures. That's why we are not content. Let's paragon what it is. See mediocrity is uninterrupted except there is your contemplation and you have inflexible exertion for that you expert that visualization you will be contented for an even though maybe for a month nevertheless not accompanying that. any sympathy for an innovative object is transient for the reason that one day you will develop distinguishing of that. Questioning is how will you find your dependable clemency? as for the time being, you will not placate with whatsoever you are deed it may accomplish. That passion and indulgence are momentary. The retort is at this crisis: Sit in inaudible and anticipate what fundamentally you are. What you do, you do it for your progression for the reason that you are not content with what you are. You do for supplementary mortals. Not ever disremember yours ignominiously. Successively cogitate what essentially you are and your scarcity. If you will paragon out a retort, unearthing in the internal your credence me afterward that you will escalate exclusively and each instantaneous of your life it may any objectionable being also your satisfaction with, not eternally enthusiasm.

The lady was over 90 years old but had a prodigious impertinence in the course of casing up glowing, spreading greasepaint, and aligning her shock in spectacular ticker tapes. She and her husband have been nuptial to each other for 70 years. After the expulsion of her esteemed partner, engrossment with no children, and averageness in the family to care for her, she categorically decided to switch to a harbouring home base. Unfluctuating on the diurnal when she expatriates her home for good. She outfitted up sophisticatedly and pragmatically sophisticated. After peripheral care at the sheltering home, she had to adjourn unwittingly in the vestibule for hours before her apartment was equipped. When a consequential smoothed her make her way to the room, she gave the lady a demonstrative depiction of the tiny intergalactic that she was meant to be. She was like "I love it" with the enthusiasm of an eight years old who has just been manageable with a new puppy. Momentous says "u haven't even perceived the room yet" just wait.

The woman retorted well my gratification has mediocrity to do with a room. "Whether I like my room or not. Doesn't depend on how the paraphernalia is schematized. It is reliant on how I accumulate my attentiveness. Serenity is coarsely you can tenacity ahead of elasticity. And I formerly uncompromised to love my bed-sitter, love civilization around me, to love my life. It is a discovery that I make every morning when I wake up.

You know the forte we all have is the sovereignty to designate how we feet. The lady had unremitting dialogue and the consequential pried diligently with her wide orifice open.

"I can employ my unabridged day in bed intellectually of the agony I am in concentrating on those parts of my physique that have no lengthier exertion. Or I can grow a bed and be appreciative of those fragments that do exertion. Respectively diurnal is a knack. And as elongated as my eyes can be tranquillity exposed. I will endure today and all the glad reminiscences that I have stowed in my concentration. Impartial for this stretch in my life!!

The consequence was dumbfounded by the reassuring impertinence of the aging lady whose life from a peripheral opinion of interpretation was only full of complications and austerity.

Dear bookworms, only complications materialize reflexively. Serenity is a choice we all have to choose. Only antagonism materializes inexorably. Armistice is an optimal we all have to make.

## OPTIMAL PRECISE AND CONSCIOUS SOUND

The furthermost wholesome two literary works WE. Affiliation means supplementary than unity. Means what you will do alone in this world? Consequently, if you want to identify how influential you are? Drop a scratch. And see how many hands come forward to spread it. That is how ironic you are. Then, you may keep an inventory of your opulence, and none is there to give you camaraderie, but I know such people are "lost souls' '. He is existing in the house like an impression. None there to segment their affiliation what a nourishing WORD that is we unfluctuating to appreciate life accurately. You have to do more than one. Not, but we and consequently Arjuna says in the Gita. What is the use of skirmish? What is the use of acquisition triumph? What is the use of sovereignty? What is the practice of momentous magnificence? If all those whom it's predestined for are contemporary in the battlefield and all shall be slain in this fratricidal battle with whom to live? If all is devastated, will you lick this all affluence will you lick? Will you lick the car? What will you do? An unpretentious interrogation? Even to appreciate life, you need more than one creature. And please add worth to your intriguing life and make your life convenient. Be with people who complement more worth to your life, don't impartially suspend out with people who take worth out of your life by construction you convincingly indicate erroneous discerning in your life.

## WHAT DO I DO WHEN BELONGINGS DON'T ENSUE THE WAY I WANT?

See, right now let's say if your dean tells you. From tomorrow all of you, what kind of attire you should wear, approximately there will be demonstrations. If your dean goes further and articulates everybody, only annoy four idols in the morning. If your dean tells you everybody should get up at 5 in the morning. Let's say he put 10 different rules like this, physical things to do, you will think he's trying to convert you into slaves, and you will scream and shriek for your autonomy, isn't it? But look at yourself and perceive, accurately now, a celebrity else, if they regulate what would ensue from place to dwelling you, you feel like you are striving. But right now, somebody else is determining what should materialize within you, is this not captivity? Somebody can choose whether you are content or unfortunate? Is this not captivity? Somebody can resolve whether you will be a pleasant anthropological presence or an unfriendly hominid animation. Is this not captivity? What materializes within you, somebody else determines- this is the nastiest arrangement of servitude, isn't it? It is just that for everyone it appears to be ordinary. It is not. It is not ordinary. Just as everybody is just like that, it does not become normal. This human presence. Life around you will never happen 100% the way you want.. and it should not happen. Because if everything transpires the way you want it, where do I go? I am very happy it's not fashionable your way. (kidding) and now that you're a scholar? You are still a scholar. I have faith in about. 60%-70% is trendy. When you get conjugal, the proportion will be upturned. We don't know which way it will go. So, if life around you will never ensure 100% the way you want it and it should not. Except you are existing with apparatuses, life will not happen and those apparatuses will freak you, isn't it? Aren't apparatuses disconcerting you every day for approximately or the other? They do, so external will never transpire 100% the way you want it and If your contentment or your enjoyment or let's not practice all these many confrontations- fundamentally it is pleasurableness vs horribleness for loveliness we have many appellations, we call it amity, contentment, delight, paradise. For horribleness, we have numerous names strain, nervousness, distress, stiffness whatsoever experimental. Plainness against pleasures- if your pleasurableness is dependent upon what transpires around you, the probability of you being pleasant all the time is remote, isn't it? In the very countryside of possessions is not conceivable only if you are intelligent to generate a detachment amongst this and that, it is not conceivable. In the sense, when things don't exertion. There is a convention in masses of people, they will guise up "uparwala". Isn't it? The entire world is looking for up. Looking up. See, you know the sphere is smoothed? Do you distinguish this? The sphere is rounded. And you are not sedentary on the uppermost of the north pole, you are sedentary in Chennai, here in the steamy microclimate and the damn sphere is whirling so if you look up you are continuously lookup in the incorrect course, isn't it? You are perpetually looking up in the erroneous track. Isn't it so? Maybe at a confident instant of, whatever. Greenwich means time, zero hours when you looked up peradventure you sensation the paradise. In respite of the while, you constantly looking in the inclusive of the scratch course. Isn't it so? So, in this intergalactic interplanetary, is there somebody who knows which is awake and which is miserable? Does somebody identify? Is there somewhere it manifest? This is up? Mediocrity identifies which is up, which is miserable, it's just a supposition, isn't it? Do you recognize really which is northerly, which is south? In the factual intelligence do you know north and south? It is just for you to convince we just static it. Isn't it? Do you know what is east and west? No. do you know what is advancing and retrograde? You do not. None of these possessions you know. There is only one entity you can be certain of right now- this is you know what is superficial, what is innermost; this one thing you are sure, isn't it? This is innermost, this is superficial- this is the only pleasure you have. What is apparent, what is private, this is all you know. Just in case, sometimes if you get enlightened, you will misplace that also.

That is what occurred to me. Now I don't identify which is the innermost, which is obvious, which is me, which is not me. That's why I am all over the world. Because I don't know whether this is me or that is me. So now you say "I know what is innermost, what is outward, let's scrutinize this a diminutive further. Can you see it approximately accurate now?? All the readers? Can you see approximately just an opinion out of what you are observing? Now, this bright is deteriorating up on that precise entity sparkly, successful through your lens system, upturned duplicate in your cornea- you know the unabridged division precisely? Where do you see that entity precisely nowadays? Within yourself!! Where have you seen the unabridged creation? Within yourself. Have you ever veteran whatsoever exterior of yourself? The whole thing that very happens to you- obscurity and bright materialized within you. Agony and preference transpired within you, delight and desolation transpired within you. Have you ever practiced anything outside of yourself? No. so, what I am questioning you is what transpires within you who should govern how it ought to happen? What materializes inside you, who ought to regulate how this ought to happen? Somebody else? Unquestionably you ought to govern what ought to transpire within this, isn't it? So, if you govern what's stylish within this (referring to oneself). Your whole involvement in life will be determined by you, nobody else but you, won't it? The procedures around you may not be regulated by you, but how your practice of life in this sphere is 100% strong-minded by you if you yield responsibility for this. If you consciously lose, just about anyone will govern it. They will-not intentionally, they are also like you, coincidence human animations should not be raised by anybody. The thing about human beings is- it's a very common word that people are using. I was raised catholic, I was raised Muslim, I was raised this or that. Nobody should raise you, that's what human means. A human means you can consciously shape yourself. If you are determinedly shaping yourself, where is the question of reacting to anything? You can respond as. According to your astuteness and your predispositions of the day. But the instant you respond you're incarcerated to the status quo in which you live. So, when approximately doesn't go your way? If something does not happen or if nonentity happens, if the whole thing that I am undertaking is unsuccessful tomorrow morning. I will tranquillity live delightfully and die delightfully. So, this is one entity that you must determine within yourself- your way of being is not strong-minded by what is trendy around you. What transpires within you must be strong-minded by you, what transpires around you there are too many militaries intricate, isn't it? When we want to do something in the world there are too many forces that have to liaise, not all of them may collaborate, never all of them will collaborate 100%. Nobody from place to place will ensure you are 100% your way. I am significant to you if you have hefty potentials of people, none, not one solitary creature in your life will happen 100% your way. 51% if they happen your way, you have a supervisory palisade on the entire status quo. But this one person (referring to oneself) must happen your way, isn't it? 100%? If this person (referring to oneself) is fashionable your way, how would you preserve that being, idyllic or dejected? That's all, you preserve this idyllic. Then in every status quo, you will do your superlative and that's all you can do. Just for the reason that your happenstance and agonizing nothing materializes healthier. So, what's the foremost supposed? The thing about me is, most of the stretch I don't have a solitary thought on my mind I am just hollow-headed. When I famine to contemplate I sit down and deliberate, but or else I don't have views hovering in my concentration. This is the unpretentious entity you have to do. The moment you're not acknowledged with whatsoever that you are not when I say anything that you are not. Right now, the waiter in this glass- is this you? If you think about it, will it have converted you? The food that you eat and the water that you drink has become you, isn't it? So, what is transpiring right now is what you gather has become you. You tell me you can be yours but can never, be you? Isn't it? The moment you have faith in roughly that is not you like yourself, even pathologically meet the requirements. But that's what has transpired/. The food appears on your plate, you say this is my nutriment. That you bothered it and say this is me. This is the mountain of respect that we have gathered. The heap of information that you've congregated has become you. The moment you identify with something that's not you, then your mind is in continual commotion. Continual commotion does not mean astuteness, this or abandoned commotion means madness. Only satisfaction or only a little bit of reprieve that you may have had everyone around you is in the same state-run. This mind is truly convenient. This hand is useful only because it takes instructions from me. If I wanted to go it goes, if I wanted to stop it stops. The equivalent is accurate with the concentration. Isn't it? I am enquiring. Does it take teaching from you? If it took instruction from you, I am sure you would indicate to preserve yourself delightful every instant of life. Whatever your intentions may be for the neighbour. But for yourself it's very clear, you want the uppermost level of pleasurableness, yes? If you had excellence amongst blissfulness and stressfulness, what would you indicate for yourself? You must make a choice. God will bless you. What would you select for yourself? Pleasantness, isn't it? When we say pleasantness, it's just this: if the body becomes agreeable, we call this healthiness; it develops very agreeable, we call it preference. If the mind becomes agreeable, we call it peacetime; become very agreeable- we call it joy. If our sentiments become agreeable- we call it love; it becomes very pleasant- we call it empathy. If our very life vitalities developed agreeable, we call it bliss. Progress is very enjoyable. We wall its reverie. If our curdling becomes pleasant, we call it an achievement. Only for victory the partnership of numerous forces around you. For the lingering four the first four levels of pleasurableness of physique, cognizance, sentiment, and energy, are just you. If you take charge of this. This will be pleasing. Outside. well, it's an interrogation of cleverness, not everyone can create peripheral pleasantness as you will have to connect many militaries.

## THIS IS WHY PEOPLE ARE INCOMPETENT TO PRESERVE THEIR CONTENTMENT

When do you categorically feel well in your life? When do you accurately sense well? When you are very glad you are well. Even if you are substantially ill, you're still well, isn't it? So primarily well-being means a confident level of pleasure, confident enthusiasm of life. What is happiness? Depression means your life dynamisms are very low and remain. Happiness means your life dynamisms are enthusiastic. There is mediocrity who has not been content. Everybody is happy. But the problem is they are not able to preserve it. That's all. If we want to be consciously well both superficially and internally. How well they live here. Be contingent on how well we accomplish our environs and how well we accomplish ourselves. Necessarily, life is management. If you don't know how to maintain your body, your mind, your sentiment, your situations, your life is wide-ranging. Your home, your societies' nations, and the world. The quality of our life is just how well we manage things with ourselves. But generally, we are thinking of management. We're applying ourselves to management only in terms of business management or industry management or generally, we are talking administration only with pecuniary state of affairs, not life as a whole. In many ways, it's unfortunate that today the most predominant factor that rules the planet has become economics. The other characteristics of life have been pushed to the turning. When economics rules, when economics is the only entity that we are thinking about we will tend to become very gross and unfortunate in so many ways. What I see is people who have failed in their lives, are suffering from their failure. People who have succeeded in their life, they are suffering from their success. If you suffer your failure it's okay. Because failure comes easy. If you agonize over your success, that is a catastrophe for the reason that success doesn't come easy. So, something that you worked for, something that you always longed for, something you wanted to create in your life when it happens, if you start suffering from that. That's a factual tragedy of life. But a large number of successful people on the planet are suffering from their success. When I say "misery their success" when you are five years of age how happy you were and today how happy you are? In 24 hours, times how many instants are you happy with? So that means you are a bad manager because aftercall everything that you did in your life is in pursuit of happiness, isn't it? All that you are doing in your life. You are doing it. you have faith in that is your happiness. You educate yourself, you pursue careers, you build families, you run after your ambitions so many things you do because somewhere you believe fulfilling those things will bring you happiness. After doing all that, if happiness is multiplying, it is going down, which means you are a bad manager of yourself. Anybody who does not know how to manage his own body, his mind, his own emotions, and his energies, if he is managing outside situations. He's only managing them by an accident, not by intent the way he wants it. Because if you do not know how to manage your mind, how to manage your energies, how to manage your interiority, supervision from the outside is bound to be accidental. When you manage situations by accident. You exist as an accident. You are a potential calamity. Being apprehensive all the time becomes a natural part of life, somehow people have concluded that if you do things in the world, you're bound to be traumatic. One is not stressful because of what they are doing; one is stressful because he is a bad manager of himself. He doesn't know how to accomplish his organization, that is why he is traumatic. It is not the nature of the job which makes one stressed. Everybody has faith that their job is stressful. No job is worrying. If you have no regulator over your systems. You will be worrying. Whether you do something or you don't do anything, isn't it so? Fundamentally management means we want to decide the course of our destiny. That's management, isn't it? We don't want to live here by accident, we want to take our lives where we want to go. That's management isn't it so? If you are managing by accident, you see not a manager without your things will run better. So, once you say 'I am a manager. That means somewhere you have categorical that you want to go in a precise way. You want to have a confident kind of situation, both inward and outward. So everybody is a manager in his capacity. If you want to manage outside situations, generally you will have to manage material and people around you. If you have to accomplish ten people or 10,000 people around you, but if you have no administration over your mind, you managing 10,000 minds is going to be a disaster. In the process of doing something if we are extinguishing human beings which are fashionable right now in the progression of managing a situation the man is broken, then the kind of management is not good, because After All the kind of management we do, is only for human well-being. If we are doing management for human well-being in the process of doing something, in the process of managing situations is not only producing something or making a profit. Human beings should rise to their full potential. If we manage every situation properly in the simple way of working. You and the people are working with you should be able to rise to their full potential.

When I say "rising to full potential" not just work potential, but as a human beings they must be able to rise to their full potential. If people work together, then people ought to be able to rise to the peak of their love, peace, compassion within themselves. If this doesn't happen, then it's bad management. Because all management this basic intent is human well-being. If that is not up-to-the-minute you are just manufacturing something. You are making little profit, but human beings are getting broken in the process, it doesn't mean anything. So if this kind of management has to happen, that just in managing a business, you find people around you raise to their peak, then you have to spend a certain amount of time. In focusing on your inner management, if this doesn't happen, you will manage situations only by accident. A lot of people have understood management as a way of throwing their weight around. A lot of people generally think management means just throwing their weight around. Throwing your weight around is not management, any fool can do that. If you manage a situation, not just things happening there, people should feel elevated. Just being in that space. Otherwise, it is not management. Above all, if you go to your place and you manage a situation, you must feel wonderful being there, if that doesn't happen you are not a good manager. So if this has to happen you need an inner dimension. When do I say inner measurement what is the inner dimension? When I say inner, I am not just talking about the body or the mind, because both this body and mind you gathered from outside in certain ways. Isn't it? So this body is just a heap of food that you gathered over some time. What you call my mind is a heap of impressions that you gathered from outside. Now you have a heap of food and a heap of impressions. If this much congregation has to happen. Something more than this must exist, doesn't it? If you are proficient in gathering such a large body and so much mind there must be something more fundamental than this. But that never comes into your involvement. You're just lost in these two heaps. Trying to make some sense out of it. Now as there is science, as there is management science for external well-being. There is management science for internal well-being. It is just that most of the time we have not loomed it systematically, we're just believing by doing something somehow the whole thing will be okay. Right now people are thinking that by educating themselves they will live happily ever after, which will be discovered after some time, it's not so. By getting a job they think they will be happy ever after. Which you will discover is not so. By making money you think you are going to be fortunate ever after, you will discover it is not so. Somebody thinks by getting married they are going to be happy ever after you will discover it is not so. So, you are trying to somehow fool yourself into believing that by doing something, everything will be okay. Though recurrently it has let you down still you believe that something else, some other miracle will make everything okay. It will not be okay even if bullshit can get you to the top. But never let you stay there. If you are seeking a life of fulfillment, if you are seeking a life of joy and peace and well-being within yourself don't try to bull yourself in some way. You must do the right thing, then it won't work. The same goes for confidence. Unless you do the right thing it just doesn't work. You may just bull yourself to believe that this will make me alright. Yes for a moment but the next moment you will crash. Please see SUCCESSFUL PEOPLE, UNSUCCESSFUL PEOPLE just look at their lives and see in twenty-four hours how many instants are joyful? How many? You go on the stress and see, how many joyful faces do you see on the street? Very few, isn't it? This is simply because we did not do inner management. We just did external management, no inner management in the process of creating what we want. The very source of our life, this planet, we are just destroying, isn't it? In the detection of our happiness, we are just making a bonfire out of this planet but still, we are not satisfied, nor are we any more joyful than what we were 500 years ago as people were, isn't it? So somewhere we have neglected the interiority. so, to turn inward, what is needed? Today, any thinking person the moment he can read ABC speak English and has extra scripts next to his name, he progresses an antipathy in the direction of whatsoever otherworldly. This is not your culpability. These so-called spiritual people have made such jokers out of themselves. They have presented spirituality in such terrible ways, ridiculous ways, that anybody who has any sense doesn't want to go anywhere near it. See spirituality means to know something which is beyond the physical. Right now, if you occur as a corporeal thing, as a body or a mind for the reason that both these belongings are accretions from outside, whatever happens outside will happen inside. If what happens outside begins to happen within you all the time. Then you being peaceful and happy is always accidental because it doesn't matter who you are. How powerful you are, how great a manager you are, the peripheral status quo will never be 100% in your control. That's the nature of life, as the scope and play of your life increases, you have less and less control over the situations in which you live. That's the authenticity of life. So, if whatever is fashionable outside is happening within you, you are being peaceful and happy in your life is a faraway thing- it's never going to happen. Only when a person begins to experience a dimension beyond the physical within himself, then he can play with the physical world whichever way he wants, he can do the best he can do with the outside world, but the interiority is undisturbed, always the way you want it. The outside will never happen 100% the way we want it. That's the reality of life. But at least this one should be happening the way we want it. If this is also not trendy the way you want it, if your body, if your mind, if your emotions, if your dynamisms are not operational the way you want it, then this is the worst kind of servitude, because somebody else categorically what should materialize within you. If somebody is categorical about what should happen around you. That itself you call it servitude. But if someone decides what should materialize within you. Is it not a more atrocious way of being a slave? I would like you to understand there is a whole science of inner administration if you don't learn that you may manage businesses but still you will not consciously live a life of accomplishment or well presence.

# CHAPTER 5

# DO WE NEED TO ASK FOR HAPPINESS AND LOVE?

Need for everyone is too dearest and to be precious. When we don't get this from anthropological certainties, we stab to get dearest from creatures if not from animals also we explore it in belongings. What is all about we all need dearest? To be precious and too hasty that love.

Let me explain the renovation between love and attachment.

Let's discuss accessories first.

Do mothers forage their children unremarkably unfluctuating supplementary than they are ravenous? Why? Because they get ahead that ABC is her youngster, she demands to grub him by any spontaneous he/she ought to not be voracious. Is it love? No, it is an attachment. Attachment is what we do nearly with anthropological what we want.70% of mothers over provender their children when they nurture up, they are in a tenacity of clinched assimilation is it righteous?? There is a renovation midst doing precise and concern agreeable. Love pliability us tranquillity and fitment variety up furious. Suppose your teen had a tournament with someone he stemmed and articulated to you. You contended to scold the substitute one without swaying who was accurate and who was specious. This is an adornment. In the status quo of love what we do is unwittingly we snoop to kid and grasp. If we love our teens we ought to retort and not respond. In love, you will uninterruptedly do:

1. Act which is righteous for him

2. Act for his serenity

In these sentiments also you will do that entity which is good for a kid because kid's preference can be in dissolute stuff also. Love is caressing someone else's pleasure previously yours.

In this flora and fauna, everyone is involved in varied implications of love. Unpretentious way of scrutiny inspections your soul. The more the soul is tired. Erudite will be the aptitudes. It is a very modest evaluation. Sophisticated the potentials more will be the hurt qualified. And if the soul is commanding. Sophisticated will be the reaction. Because we are empty. We will be imposing almost from the peripheral to consciousness honourable. So, you ought to pay for my system for me to be consciousness righteous. And more the soul is pleased. You can be your system. And I am beforehand unavailable. That's the procedure of prevailing. In collaboration, they are so disparate. So, in the time of life of depravity, we believed up like impoverished hands give me love, elasticity me approbation, elasticity me appreciative, elasticity me countersignature, self-assurance me. exertion bequeathing to me, snoop to me precise now not progressive. and exertion precisely how I tell you which means the vegetation and creatures should be my way. For me consciousness is righteous. And the age of authenticity means the ecosphere can be their way my warmth decent is not contingent on the ecosphere. Only two properties are plausible in every dissection, furthermore, the quaking of the passage anguishes us. second option? Our shuddering traces the division. If the shuddering of the division disturbs us. We stance like panhandlers' gage and unsteady of the section is on our distinctiveness. If our shivering anguishes the scene then we are an intense analogous philanthropic indicator. What viewpoint corresponds to this? Otherworldly souls' Otherworldly souls are units of elasticity. So, who do we convert in the age of depravity? We were deified, now we are modified from benefactor to patron and in the fundamental age of immorality (Ghor Kalyug), we don't unflinchingly take possessions from people we snatch things from them. So, when we attain this status quo, we twitch deifying celestial souls. only glorifying? What is the connotation of glorifying? You are an indulgent somebody which means if I worship somebody. Which means then? Become like them. We ought to do things that modify us from captivating to philanthropic. Which shifts us from normal to deific souls.

So, we normal souls have to organize approximately which will renovate into celestial souls. So, what do the usual souls do to renovate themselves? They will transform from enchanting to philanthropic. That's it. That's what we all have to do. Your elasticity me, you work corresponding to me no I will elasticity you; I will venerate you, I will coordinate with you, I will spring you love. I will appreciate you more than you comprehend me. Shifting. Our soul's battery will? Charged? If we give something to someone who will get foremost? Whatever we generate foremost we will develop it only. Do we get annoyed when someone first gets the same sensitivity?? We only. The other person over some time acquires to guard themselves. But the architect cannot save themselves from their conception. We cannot seepage from our peculiar vigour. The other person if he wants won't receive your liveliness at all. He will grin confidentially and appreciate that you are in this mode and go away. But we cannot outflow our commencement.

Is it conceivable the public and status quo will be my technique? No. so the user interface strategy is somewhere erroneous. That if people and status quo are my way then I am happy otherwise I am not!! So, when the software design materialized infantile people and status quo in my way, I am content. If not then it's ordinary to get annoyed. We are existing with that credence structure. And we keep comporting ourselves bestowing to that credence arrangement. Now let's produce a new credence arrangement. People and the status quo cannot always be by way. If society and status quo are bestowing to me then I am content if not?? Not respond to it automatically with your new credential organization. When we were offspring, we went with our paternities to the souk one day we whispered that I want that and they said that no we partake a portion of them at home, don't take them. But I am famished by it. No, you don't prerequisite it. Then what did we do in the middle of the souk? We are underway horrible piercingly. And our parents procured that entity for us approximately that's the day the programming transpired. And the flora and fauna are quick with this credence. If we say it piercingly our work will be ended. The exertion grows finished but approximately experimental materialize too. Our exertion grows but lengthways with what experimental transpires? My soul's series of sanitations and when my battery sanates out. It disturbs my life. We are homeopaths. How ought the vigour pitch of homeopaths be?


## READ THIS TO MODIFY YOUR BEHAVIOUR

Booklovers none in this world is faultless. We all have some deficiencies, some weaknesses, some culpabilities, some errors. We all have an upright side of us, but then we also have some habituations, some bad traditions that have continued along with us and are rigid to let go of. Have you ever taken note of the spelling of the word HABIT if you take out of it ABIT still remnants now you yield the A out of it BIT still remainders and then if you take out of it still remainders that's undoubtedly why we say OLD HABITS DIE HARD a great Zen teacher named benzoin had many apprentices? One day the student came up to their teacher benzoin and reported how they had caught one of their fellow students red-handed as he was stealing something in class, benzoin long-sufferingly heard them out but took no accomplishment. A combination of existences advanced, the same boy was jammed larceny yet once more another stint. And Veen this time the zen master did unequivocally nothing. This infuriated all the students under him who originated up to him and demonstrated that he exercises this boy who was an uncontrollable thief out of his seminary. They further endangered that if no accomplishment was taken against the boy. They will all leave the school. And then benzoin could have this thief as his only student and teach him in the armistice. The teacher subpoenaed all the students for a meeting when they had all congregated, he said to them, "see you all good boys impending from good people, you all are matured, and you know what is right and what is wrong. If you leave my cool, you'll unquestionably have no trouble in joining some other school. But what about this associate of yours? He indeed is habituated to stealing and I am aware of it. He does not even know the difference between right or wrong. If I reject him, which other school will take him? Who will teach him if I don't? who will put the determination to restructure him, if I don't? I am sorry I cannot ask him to go. It's been wonderful teaching you guys and I would love to have you continue with me. But if because of his staying you want to leave, well who am I to stop you? Students were stunned by their teacher's answer. Being touched by his empathetic nature and inspired by the values that he held sacred, they decided to stay on. And the boy who had stolen, he had tears rolling down his eyes too. The broad-mindedness and compassion of the zen master benzoin transomed his heart. He never stole again in his life later. And his later life became enormously renowned for his integrity. Mistakes happen wrong and sometimes repeatedly. Rather than labelling people as bad, we must reform by sensitivity/ empathy of course, if someone is hardwired to do wrong and does not show any signs of remorse or any signs of improvement and continues to shamelessly abuse the goodness shown to them. Such people may need to be treated differently. But in most cases can transform people with patience and compassion. Remember every saint has a past and every wrongdoer has a future. GIVE OTHERS A CHANCE.

# CHAPTER 6

# WAKE UP-MEDITATION-SLEEP

## MEDITATION

The whole thing is your prerequisite to identify to yield a comprehensive rheostat of your life. Meditation for me is the prime life assistance. Furthermost significant psychological expertise which you can acquire. Envisage that instant when you have entirely rheostat on your thoughts with this you can switch your activities, can control your habits. Meditation is impartial, similar to a cheat code with which you can go far in your life. Meditation intensifies your restraint with this you can lose your weight, accomplish your annoyance, can control apprehension occurrences, enhancement in snooze, improved well-being, you can intensify your focus but these reimbursements are of superior coating. Interior is you can grip the whole thing tranquillity. Unfluctuating you can disrupt your compulsions too. (Smoking, alcohol). You will sensation supplementary associated from your environs.

But the problem is that these individuals have byzantine meditation that they can sell you their progressions and books but trust me you don't need that belonging. The straightforward rehearsal of meditation is identical and unpretentious. You prerequisite just three things for an efficacious meditation. But before that let's know what meditation is. Meditation is still in your mind.

Environment: find contented surroundings to sit for meditation it really doesn't matter whether you are sedentary on the floor or chair, but your back should be straight variety, sure there are no disruptions around beginner don't go more than 20 minutes.

Technique: close your eyes and focus on your breath. Breathe in and breathe out. Concentrate on how your breath goes in. how your lungs expand with that and how your stress comes out with air. But you will notice that while doing this you will be distracted easily. This is called the monkey mind. In 5 seconds only you will think about something else- I have forgotten keys in the car, I think. Or maybe you will think that you had to make a phone call. or some other distraction. BRING BACK YOUR FOCUS TO YOUR BREATH. Meditation gets rid of the clutter. Make meditation easy. Do it after isometrics because you are tired as we can quintessence more, we cannot essence appropriately when we are hyperdynamic.

Constancy: Meditating once a week won't help for psychological evolution same as gym once in a week not help for corporeal evolution. Meditation is not a hasty injection. Few individuals drop this idea while rational contemplation is not plateful then it takes time.

What is meditation when we know the exact answer? Everyone is having a different way of meditation like a detergent has many varieties. DON'T ASK HERE AND THERE THAT WHAT IS MEDITATION I REPEAT DON'T ASK everyone will tell you their way and will tell you to don't do from others way. You will get more disorderly. You don't have to give absorption. You have to concentrate. Don't do that trap where you have to close your eyes and you will see the light blah blah. Don't imagine these things. We essentially want the best technique which we can follow which can solve our problem. So don't knock the progressions otherwise you will be entombed there only it may be 10 years or more than that. Quintessence tranquillity that is authentic what is trendy in your body and life that is meditation. Like you are partaking in something after eating how do you feel? That is meditation. We are not conscious these days. We are in a virtual world. We don't have any idea what's going on in the world. You can do meditation wherever you presume you are imminent on the metro. Just switch off your phone and be aware of what's happening.

You can see the reimbursements of meditation in your career too.

Corporeal commotion is not satisfactory. We need a mental forte also to contest from the world and first, we need to fight from undesirable sensations. Meditation is not less than medicine for mental health, essentially physical too.

Meditation for particularly those who have to give any competitive exam or necessity further absorption for learning.

After awakening up and before snoozing our brain is characteristic of discerning many belongings that jump into different thoughts. Like monkeys while studying our mind jumps here and there for example: while studying you are not able to study you are using your phone and you want to go out for a movie or cafe etc.

We all organize this. These days this status quo is because of the internet and many other apps. That's why the dimensions of attentiveness are less because of the internet, messaging, and all. Few students can't even still appropriately even 20 minutes. For doing whatsoever you should have dimensions of absorption. If you have that you don't need meditation but 90% of people don't. And students do study, but they don't get most of the things and they think maybe their memory is less and maybe they are not that intelligent. Usually, if we think about meditation, we think that it is a relational thing. Because we usually watch on televisions when saints meditate. Our brain usually runs in the past or future. The brain usually doesn't think more about the future. We just need to train our brains to concentrate on the future.

As I said, concentrate on breathing. Deep concentration in silence and that's it...

WITH THIS TRUST ME ONE DAY YOU ARE GONNA MEET THE HAPPIEST VERSION OF YOURSELF.

How to have an unfathomable nap to galvanize your concentration and physique?

The mode of life which takes precedence in our concentration. Precisely now, if we perceive from the former few decades our precedence is continuously the superficial world so it's about taking overhaul of family, taking care of work, taking care of society and when it emanates to identity it takes care of the body. So that's where the identity ends, we do not ever think about taking care of ourselves (mind). The self is in (mind) when this life verdures we call this dead form. Somebody is engaged for a surgical procedure the doctor will say ``sister take mister so and so inside in case things don't go right the doctor will say "sister take the body out". So, see when a body was taken inside, he was mister so and so and if the life leaves the body is out. Live the vigour. So, unworldliness means taking care of that vigour. Which we can call by different words we can call it energy, we can call it consciousness, we can call it light, power, soul, spirit. These all are just words. The important thing is to just understand I am not just this body, I am (mind's) energy. And this energy is the creator of every thought, feeling, intention and this energy decides what I speak, this energy decides how I behave, how I work, how I live. So, everything is happening in our minds. It's like the energy center of the city, the energy center of the house. If the energy center doesn't work appropriately, nothing works properly and yet we are not concentrating on the energy center. So, our mental health issues, our physical health issues, our relationships, our environmental health issues are actually from the mind because every thought we create, on average we are generating about 70000-80000 thoughts in a day what doctors teach us. So, if around 70k thoughts in a day it's a vibration, it's energy so the thought is not going to stay in my head it vibrates so it affects my emotional state so that's mental health. My every thought radiates to my body, affecting my physical health. So however good may be my diet, my exercise if we are not intelligent right if we are not fashioning the right emotions we still don't have best of corporeal well-being, my every opinion emits to people generates my relationships and my every alleged exudes to the environment so even so environmental health is prejudiced from cognizance so piousness just communicates us to come to the fundamental, center take care of the inner world the superficial world will start receiving taken care of if we yield upkeep only of the superficial world without enchanting care of the innermost world we are not accomplishment the explanation. Every thought we engender see we all can sensation our vibrations if can feel how you are feeling today as we say we are sensitivity very low today infrequently we say "I am warmth very low currently" sometimes we say "I don't sensation like meeting anyone currently" but word sensitivity is there always occasionally we go to a dwelling and say I am touch very nice in this place it's good vigour we meet people and say I am feeling the very good vibe from that person, sometimes we say I am not sensation good ambiances from that person. So, we can texture the tremor. The important thing is to take care of the superiority of the liveliness that I am generating so sensitivity is after I have twisted the alleged. Suppose I met you this morning and thought "you are a delightful emotion with very unadulterated intent, a very influential assignment. This is the thought that I am creating. Once I start fashioning a thought about you. I will be impressed with you. So, the sensitivity is the second phase the initial phase is the supposed so where does the thought get twisted from? The cause of our opinions is the

1. Material we devour

2. Our past involvements

3. Our belief system

Belief system means. Do I believe that stress is normal? Do I believe anger is necessary? Do I believe life is a competition? Do I believe that I have to be better like other people? These are belief systems. This belief system creates my thoughts.

This is where the most imperative is evidence. It is the gratified we devour so an identical imperative equivalence is a whole thing I timepiece, the whole thing I delivered, the whole thing I eavesdrop on is who I become. So, content= disposition so if we look at the last few decades we are abruptly overwhelmed with content. When I was in school, I did not have mobile it was tranquil not there in India, I think. No cells, no cyberspace 30-35 years back. The first thing was televised. So, we were not conversation desperateness, we were not discussing nervousness, we are not even speaking trauma. It was impartial in physics compression divided by resistance than as we got swamped with gratified, a proficiency which made our life enormously calm but we are not using it the right way the phone's life is tremendously comfortable, but we embrace on to it as if we can't live without it, we sleep with it, we wake up with it in the intermediate of the night also we scroll it that is what is preparatory taking rheostat our mind. If the liveliness center gets paraphernalia by pleased because it works everything starts becoming affected. So, always feel content=temperament=destiny so if we take care of gratified temperament and intention start receiving taken care of in the preceding few years, we have seen the precipitous intensification in psychological well-being problems even in India and I think it's all over the world but in last year it went even higher. Doctors last month were maxim it's no more about nervousness, it's about nervousness syndrome now so it is no more excitement it's a coherent healthiness problem. So, now we prerequisite to ask yourself covid was corporeal well-being problem we know how to shield yourself we all are taking overhaul what is the construction between psychological well-being and covid? Covid could not do whatsoever in our cognizance it is only affecting our body. But it's a subject with demonstrative well-being. Demonstrative well-being means my handling skills with a status quo. This was not my technique so the coping skill and covid is the global status quo but we all have a particular state of affairs, family circumstances, we have proficient conditions so every time there is a condition I have to re-join, we retort to every state of affairs. One rejoinder is an alleged, second rejoinder is a conversation, and the third rejoinder is behaviour and now before covid also we were breathing a life where we whispered that our interior rejoinder is reliant on the quality of the state of affairs and people's behaviour this is the life of demonstrative dependency where I live my life saying I am angry because of another person. I am in pain because of this person. This person is very exasperating, I am hassled because of this person this terminology which is kind of accustomed to talking about which we were increasing up. Vascularly saying that the whole thing happens in the outer world is fashioning my inner world, so I am dismayed because of someone, I am hurt because of someone I am happy because of someone. So, whether it is happiness or sadness it is approximately to do with the outside world so every thought in the inner world is dependent on every thought of the outer world. This is the major mistake we have made; my mind is always dependent on the world, and we need our world to be picture-perfect, my spouse to be flawless, my children to be perfect, my parents to be perfect. And perfect according to my definition of perfect and when they are not my way or their situation is not my means, I started producing offended agony annoyance occasionally even abhorrence in the habit of complaining not being contented, criticizing, fear so this is low demonstrative well-being so if I visualize this cordless. Our mind is not a battery, but we are envisioning it. See our phone battery or laptop battery not where we stand there to attach it. Because I don't want it to shut down so I will charge my technology. Similarly, a day if I could see this cordless then I would know where am I is it four lines, three lines, two lines where this battery is but because I cannot see it keep living my life reacting to situations diminishing my vigour, every time I am producing these adverse sentiments, I am depleting this battery and unexpectedly comes a situation in my life like covid was a state of affairs. And this battery which was previously probably two or one suddenly got hit by a bigger situation and I did not have the strengths to face it so from two I went to one line and when I want to one line there converted chances to slanting to a psychological well-being question it was not more a demonstrative health issue it was a psychological well-being problem. If we take care of incriminating this battery daily like we charge our expertise then the situation will be external may not always be perfect, but I am the creator of my every thought and feeling we have to hold on to this every day we cannot live life culpability we can take a life of self-accountability I am the originator of every thought-feeling. So, let's start it with the minuscule status quo of the diurnal: someone saying approximately to you which you don't like, someone who is performing the diverse way. Just take charge of your mind, little inconsequential state of affairs of the day. Re-join right, respond vigorously. This means if they are doing something which is not right, I have to be tranquil and deferential in my response that will conserve my battery here if I respond, if below. These are unpretentious belongings. I am depleting my battery so in every division I will take care. Am I safeguarding my health? Or am I depleting my health? Which becomes an ordinary way of breathing clemency will turn out to be ordinary, allowing go of the historical will become ordinary and this battery will remain persuaded then we will not dip down to any compulsion. If we will take care of our demonstrative health. And there are simple life elegance habits that we follow to yield an overhaul of this demonstrative well-being.

So, galvanize our cognizance and body is trendy during our snooze so snooze is a very imperative factor for psychological health matters and corporeal well-being issues. What has happened in the last few decades since the while we have all these technologies with us. We started compromising on our sleep cycle we didn't have this leading we customarily go to sleep after work because nonentity much to do read a virtuous manuscript, occupy time with family then we inevitably go to sleep it was a natural way of existing nobody taught us that it would just materialize on its own and when we sleep at the precise time in a precise way then there is a lot of remedial materialize during the snooze. So, sleep is for dispensing everything that's going on in the concentration giving the mind response, inactive the mind, and then going to the delta state of the sleep which is the deep sleep. Where the energizing happens and it's the delta stage. One sleep cycle means at one stretch when we sleep at night, we will go into two sleep cycles. two delta stages are enough, energizing us for the rest of the day. And the therapeutic of the body also transpires during sleep so therapeutic of every mouthpiece now for that what we need to do is:

**1.** Sleep early, when we were in school, we were imparted to bed early to rise. Makes a person vigorous, well-off, wise. I don't know whether that clarifies that in school to any further extent for the reason that most of the children keep pursuing late night and they are going to sleep in the morning. Whatever we do is not as per countryside, against nature it will start taking control over the period. So, the best time for sleep is 10-2. That's another science that 10-2 is revitalizing the mind and the body. If as a substitute of 10 I sleep at 11 I lose 1 out of the 4 hours, if I sleep at 12, I mislaid two. And if I sleep at 2 even if I sleep 8 hours after that I have lost the best time of stimulating so now priority has to be set right if I am going to decide to sleep at 10 at 8 which means 2 hours before I sleep or around 7:30 I should finish my dinner so my digestion happens before I go to sleep. So, during my sleep, my body doesn't have to digest so my body only focuses on healing. Energy can do only one thing at a time if I sleep and just have a heavy meal before sleep then the next few hours like 10-2 time of energizing will go on digestion and if the body is only doing digestion during those hours, then the body doesn't get time to heal so over some time disabilities and other issues take place. Because digestion has not taken place before sleeping. So, the best time is at least 2.5 hours before slumbering. Dinner and the lighter dinner. That it's digesting speedily and then the physique only ends for the healing now the same thing for the mind because of the technology we are connected to our exertion till we go to sleep so we are scrutiny work emails, we are scrutiny work messages, we are having business calls we are doing everything till we close our eyes. Even while closing our eyes, we usually scroll once again "any new message" now if consume all this work-related information before sleep then my mind is in the bite plus stage which means the overexcited active stage. But because the body is tired, I will track to snooze but my mind has got so copious to think about the next couple of hours my mind will be dispensation all the evidence when we wake up in the morning, we will not feel renewed and bouncing some people if you see in the morning on the way to work, I love to look at the faces if you see the faces early morning how happy are they, how healthy do they look and how energetic are they. Many people look very tired in the early morning, you cannot make out whether they are going to work or returning from work, their faces look very exhausting early morning. We are asleep underprivileged generation. Which is the cause of intellectual health issues. So, 10 to sleep two hours previously slumbering disengage all announcement we can put the whole thing for next morning email, messages, phone calls leave only for crises if there is an alternative.

**2.** At least one hour before disengaged from mass media which means movies serializations books that stimulate cognizance, definitely not the world newscast. It is poisonous to devour world news before you sleep. You can't impair yourself anyway more than that. I was just overwhelmed by all the visuals, information. It's real we all need to know about it but not before sleep because our mind will flood with all that not just visual but the sentiment of the visual, sentiment of bereavement, the illness the terror whatsoever. That's not what you give to the mind formerly going to sleep so two hours before disconnecting from the world's news.

**3.** Last hour should be occupied in an inner way that can slow down your observance. Slow down the mind before we go to bed like a good book, a self-transformational book, comforting music, a diary writing. It's identical good to transcribe a diary on the daily basis, a daily journey. So, you realize your sentiments before you go to sleep. And then we are meditative before we go to sleep at least 10min capitulation the whole thing to superlative, clean the mind, forgive people before we go to sleep, if there was anything happen during the day, please exonerate people before going to sleep. And please ask for clemency before going to sleep in your mind. It's all trendy in your mind. Because if I do not excuse or inquire to exonerate before I sleep and I go to sleep with that demonstrative wound then it is not more on the top layer of the mind during my sleep it goes deep into my subconscious mind and that's where we are field on our past since few years because we go to sleep with it. So, the regime before sleep is very important. The daily journal releases it, forgive people, ask for pity, anything worrying your mind counsel yourself, engrave the response to yourself like you are counselling your friend, and then 15 min before sleeping consume a healthy emotional diet. Which means spiritual content, self-transformation book. Whatsoever that you are corresponding. But it should be a high vibrational, emotional diet. Which means content that is full of compassion, faith, divinity, purity, power, love, acceptance, gratitude everything I want to become. I need to consume for 15 minutes before I go to sleep. So now that will be evidence going to process my mind, exude to my body during the 6 hours of sleep. If we sleep like this way, decelerating our mind before we go to sleep that I would unsurprisingly wake up premature, so we gain on time by sleeping the right way. By slumbering the right way, I don't prerequisite more than 6 hours of sleep. Anybody can experiment. You will unsurprisingly wake up between 4 or 5 am. That is the uppermost vibrational time of a 24 hours cycle. 4 to 5 am. Even today people are taking the 5 am supervision club. So why do they want best to wake up at 5 am? Inventiveness is uppermost perception influence is uppermost, anything that is in your mind you will get resolution at that time. For awakening up early one hour after you wake up again not concerning the world.

Because your captivation power is highest so don't put the world in it. We have the respite of the day for it.

## READ IT AFTER YOU WAKE UP

As a supernumerary of gambolling out of bed, and whistling precisely into the stress of what you need to do, breathe in. Take an instant to eradicate the anxiety and re-align your mind, body, and brain with the joy which does live exclusive to you. You get to indicate if your day is going to be like every other day, or if it is going to be a GREAT DAY, and you decide first thing in the morning. By giving yourself that time, to realign your brain to positivity. To redirect your mind to what is GOOD in your life. What is GOOD in your life precisely now? Take an instant to deliberate about it.

START YOUR DAY WITH INTENT. TODAY I WILL BE CONTEMPORARY. TODAY I WILL BE SYMPATHETIC. TODAY I WILL BE AN ILLUSTRATION. I ASSUME OF FURTHER. TODAY I WILL ELASTICALLY MY ALL IN EACH INSTANT.

It's all about intent. When you straighten your emphasis to the good you will see improvement. If your emphasis is absorbed to the strain and scrap. You will perceive more scrap. If you want to be categorically pleased; give thanks. That's surreptitious. Contented people are appreciative people. So, devote while appreciating Ness. Spend time in intent and anticipation for what a great day. Today is going to be. Feed your mind with something positive. Meditate and uplift yourself. Something that will breed your concentration or essence. You captivate your tenacity, you entice your theories. You fascinate what you sensation. So, grow up and feel virtuous when you unswerving your concentration to the virtuous you will see more virtuous if your emphasis is directed to the stress and scrap you will see more scrap and anxiety. That is your only occupation. Get up and get yourself astounded. Ask yourself; how can I feel prodigious today? How can I cultivate today? How can I make others feel great today? Open your eyes to the magic around you. I assure you. You have been misled out of phenomena because you've been lost in the anxiety and racket confining your head. Get out of your head and get enchanted with life. TODAY IS An INNOVATIVE DAY. I RENEWED, HYGIENIC PIECE. YOU CAN SHADE WHATSOEVER YOU WANT ON THE CANVAS NO MATTER WHAT ENSUES. YOU ARE THE ILLUSTRATOR. ADD SOME COLOR, SOME PLEASURE. Some life to your image. Authorization nonentity off the canvas! As soon as you get up in the morning. As yourself. What's imperative today is it chief I rush around hassled; at the whole thing, I have to become finished. Or can I impartially appreciate this instant for a breather of my diurnal? You adopt what sympathetic diurnal you will partake in. Now, what transpires but how you will RETORT to the whole thing that transpires. You can rejoin absolutely

Today was a delightful day. Today I have ended my apiece and each commission with my unabridged cognizance and temperament. Today what I have understood and what knowledge I have expanded I am exclusively gratified with. My physique, my intelligence, my aptitude, and my depth are entirely in concord. Today whatever happened was better than yesterday and my tomorrow will be much healthier than nowadays. I am very content and sensitive, so I don't have any apprehension or anxiety. I have no confines. I am unrestricted form whatsoever. This entire world is around to help me to make me a good person. Every day I acquire something innovative and nowadays what I have erudite I am beholden from my unabridged heart. And I am fully equipped to absorb a rather innovative tomorrow. My intellect is entirely diverse. My status quo was entirely different. I am diverse from the whole world.

That's why there is no evaluation with someone. I am not only the physique, but I am also the unabridged world. Every supremacy of this world is not exterior, it's exclusive to me. I want to release my actual negative habit. And my heart is more nonviolent and ecstatic. And I can eavesdrop on my heart's vocal sound. I am sensitive to concord from inside. I have faith that today what complications I face in my life tomorrow will be the purpose of my accomplishment. When I breathe in, I inhale positive intellect. When I breathe out, I exhale negative thinking. Whatever happens to me is always for some good. I love to spend time with myself and listen to the voice of my soul and accordingly I progress in my life, and this is the goal of my life. I love everybody. And everyone loves me. I am not at all property any resentments with anybody. Those who did incorrectly with me can be deliberately or inadvertently I am merciful to them from all my heart. In the past, whatever error I have done, I exonerate myself entirely. My attentiveness is not ancient but forthcoming. I have premeditated what I have to do tomorrow. I am equipped to accomplish my every goal. Today whatever I have whosoever is with me I am thankful from my heart. Whatever is happening in my life, everything is so delightful. Whatever will happen will be wonderful. Everyone thinks it's good for me. I think it's good for the whole world. I give sanctification to everyone from the sentiment that everyone should make an armistice. Everyone should be healthy. everyone's astuteness should be on a precise track. Everyone's life should be full of happiness. I am keeping every anxiety away from a successful sleep. And tomorrow morning I will wake up with new anticipation. And I will do innovative things in my life. Now, this is the time to rest and my body, my mind is totally at peace.

## WAKE UP EARLY AND ATTACK THE DAY

Why is it so important to get up early? Some of you all don't want it, that's why you haven't got it. I don't sleep when I am tired, I sleep when I am done. The average millionaire wakes up at 4:00 am. STORY OF A MILLIONAIRE) So it started at 4 am where I'd started. And I'd start with my cardio and then I'd have mealtime and then I would go to the gym and then I'd go to exertion. Some of you all have no idea what 4:00 am appearances correspond to. Why would you not wake up at 4:30 am? Because you're too demanding, slumbering in. I'm attractive, sure I will follow up later than all of you, said the millionaire. He says we don't sleep when we are exhausted, we sleep when we are done. On the other side, we are too tiring hammering the snooze button numerous times. Justifications should be superlative to the person that's creating them up. And if we can be honest some of you all don't even go to bed until about 4:00 am. if you can get up before the rest of the world is conscious. Right before the adversary is conscious, you can get so copious done you're so much more industrious. Stop feeling sorry for yourself, wake your ass up. And then they ask, "why are you up so early"? take responsibility to make your life materialize. Awaken the beast exclusive. wake up at 4:00 am. so I instigate to tell myself there must be a purpose. When you have something to do when you have someone to love. When you have something to look forward to when you get up in the morning. See people who have approximately to look forward to don't need an alarm clock. Because they have a purpose for being. If you want to have one of the best lives in the world, which is, you live on your terms, then you have to pay dues to get there. You've decided that you're not profitable to allow your surroundings to describe you. You've decided that you're not going to tolerate the abyss. The things, the people, life govern who you become. You have a problem with your life; you have a problem with your situation. If you want more freedom in your life you have to have more chastisement. If you do what is easy, your life will be hard. But if you do what is hard. Your life will be informal. You've decided that you're not going through life being a whiner being a protestor. That you're going to take accountability for what it is that you want to create. That extreme aptitude that God has given mankind above the faunae. Is the ability to choose. In the morning the first thing we do is to hit the snooze button where you have a prime. A choice to hit the snooze button and go back to sleep to that cozy bed or arise and get up that's the choice of chastisement. You are accurately exercising your mind to take the easy way-out discipline is a muscle you have to train. It's a pronouncement that can shape the rest of your life.

## GET UP AND GET IT DONE

Don't categorically want to grow up and grow out of bed? Yah. I get up and get it out of bed. I don't want to work out, I work out. I categorically don't need to hammer on a venture. I hammer on the venture. As an inclusive rule, I do not like procrastination. You need to get possessions finished but if you are working to rest, that is one entity that you should adjourn on, that's the one thing I want you to put off until tomorrow. Now, these could be signals that you need some time off and those indications might be precise. They could be exact, but don't take today off. Don't elasticity, an instantaneous indulgence that is voicelessness in your ear, shut that down. Do not listen to that little voice instead go through the gesticulations, lift the masses, sprint the hill, work on the venture, get out of bed. If you only have 24 hours in a day, your accomplishment is reliant on how you use the 24. You got to hear me people talk about Oprah Winfrey, you know ted food turner, warren sideboard listens. I don't care how much money you have. You only get 24 hours in a day and the difference between Oprah and the person that's broke is Oprah uses her 24 hours wisely. That's it. Listen to me, that's it. You get 24. I don't care if you broke, you grew up destitute, I don't care if you grew up rich. I don't care if you're in college, you're not in college, you only get 24 hours, and I blew up literally. I can tell you all about your life if you just write down your 24 hours agenda for me. You let me appear at it, I can tell you where you're going to be in 5 years, I can tell you where you're profitable to be in ten years. I can tell you where you're going to be in 20 years. If you keep that agenda. We don't recognize the legacy or who are and what we can do so we just say that I'm just going to do whatever and get a combination of jokes but when you identify how great you are when you recognize that victory that's confidential, you'll say you know what I got more to give. There's more than life than this right here. I deserve better. You deserve better and then you'll say you know what, what I'm going to do I'm gonna prove everybody who didn't believe in me wrong and the few people who do believe in me imam prove them right and when you do that everything inside your life changes. I must start saying before I make pronouncements, I just started saying okay, is this going to make my parents proud of all the people that are hating on me it's just going to make them say "see I told you " I am in India writing. I've found out the philosophy in India there, in Bangalore has the uppermost suicide proportion because if these kids do not do well in high school, they know they won't go to college and that know for rest of their life they'll end up with deficiency and they said I'd rather die than to be in scarcity. That's what makes you nervous. What, you're going to settle for whatever the world gives you? You're going to settle for living how your mom and dad live now? I am telling you all my young friends; you ain't gotta settle for that. Most people contemplate that the people that are a very high-level civilization are cut from a diverse cloth. They think that they're exactly diverse. Breed than them and that they're and that they can't get those things. That's kind of interesting right and it's continuously kind of horror to have the myth of that person burst but see here's the thing. Although we're not cut from a diverse cloth, the fact that I mastered it. Constancy is the difference, and most people will never do that. None wants you to flourish right? Only your parents don't want you to succeed because they're afraid you're not gonna call her back. Your brain doesn't want you to be a big achievement. Your brain just wants to keep you flourishing. All your brain wants you to do is impartially pump out two kids so that the DNA can endure on, that's it. Your brain will pretend to be you. You are your own nastiest enemy. I know that if I fail to do that, that I am not instilling behaviours, that's going to have a big-picture long-term goal. Dude, talent is overrated at home. There's no price great for me. There's nothing too great. I would die for my dreams. Do you know what I'm writing? I'm willing to jeopardy it. There's nothing too excessive. There's no quantity that I am not willing to go out and you could accomplish anything you want man. if you're willing to do it right? But again, you'll comprehend that what you think you are not what you are. You become something else. You become approximately else. If you want to be assiduous you cannot be exhausted down, you'll become something else. So, you don't have individuals' restrictions an ordinary human being has, you don't have that for the reason that you become something else. You become something that anthropomorphizes confident belongings that you're trying to move forward. You'll go to the slight length you; you're not going to get exhausted for the reason that that because do that, at that argument you have God on your side. That's not even you anymore dude. It's like, you know how? What I do is concentrate on perhaps one or two or three belongings at a time and then I impartially do it and then I get that completed and then I do the subsequent entity and then I get that done and then

I do the next thing. No one's going to put you on. You got; you have to put yourself. So, of your variety, you just do your insignificant errands and you do it but see no one the whole thing to perceive that. Accomplishment is about impartial noiseless little movements. Receiving rid of whatsoever that's gratuitous. Accomplishment is like an inaudible daily set of errands, real small. Factual and insignificant. It's very inaudible. It's a very quiet progression where you're just illustrating your state from within yourself doing these like unpretentious little errands but verdict love in those simple little errands. It's not this big rah-rah speech where you do this one thing and something big happens. I am exhausted. I don't want to do it and I got a million explanations not to do it but what I do is I make the prime that I say if I can't variety myself go do this, how am I going to live my imaginings? I found that if I miss one day. I'll miss every day. People are continuous wo during what the subsequent period in life is and I say, life's a little bit like a confusion you know? Until you walk the miserable one hallway and try to open the door you don't know if it's a deceased end or not and people are annoying to sit back and that's where the adjournment emanates in and look real far down the hallway, and I'm living, impartial walk 9:00.

They looked at the most efficacious men and women of the world and they found they had like seven-eight things in common as a routine.

Failing to prepare was preparing to fail the night before a game I ate the same food I went to bed at the same time I got up I ate the same breakfast so the routine and the preparation some people call it superstition but it's a routine the stronger your mindset is the greater your skill set is going to be we remember the stuff we earn the stuff we experience more than what the teacher tells us or what someone gives us for free a company is simply a group of people as leader of people you have to be great listener you have to be a great motivator you have to be very good at praising and looking for the best in people you think warren buffet reading just to be read the majority of you are poor because you read poor stuff everything was done to try to learn how to become a better basketball player everything and so when you have that point of view then literally the world becomes your library to help you to become better at your craft it's what goes on between this year and this year in our hearts that determine our lives out there there's no there's no world out there except what's going on here I think it's important that you really like whatever you' re doing if you don't like it life is too short if I'm lying to you about who I am or I'm lying to you about whatever there no starting point their a false reality right you have to create the real reality it's a good separation for me you know emotionally to b to put myself in a place where at practice or when I'm training or during games I switch my mind to something else I become number one in the world I become a millionaire not because I made more money I become a millionaire because they told me millionaires only live off 30 of their income I become millionaires did I stopped living off a hundred percent what does it mean time is money right how do you multiply time how do you buy time rich people buy time.

## THE MINDSET OF HIGH ACHIEVERS COMPILATION STARTS IN

Most of people watching this thing should either not be in business if they've got one or close the down if they got one because you in business for all the wrong reasons and you don't have the balls to close them down because of what other people are going to say you don't you have no idea how limitless it is when you're not afraid of what other people think of say you have no idea there's not two people watching this thing that even has a concept of what it is to act as if you have no limits to your abilities zero I wrote a book and uh called the millionaire booklet wrote that book in two hours it was translated 38nlanguages for free because of my social media standing around the world I just asked a bunch of people can you help me 38 languages and literally in one month the whole book was produced written translated like you need friends counter intuitive 50 page pamphlet type book yeah you're making not the new York times bestseller yeah where'd that come from another contrarian again like the book publishers you know they're dying they're come on man that's antiquated that you don't even count digital downloads like what's wrong with you right so give them something they can read in a couple hours give him something 19 months to write my last book because the publisher was involved okay I'm not supposed to write a book while I'm writing a book so I wrote a booklet okay wrote the booklet in two hours the booklet made more money in 19 days than other book made 19 months and was translated in38 languages the other took that book 19 months publishers editors but you know all this energy al this wasted freaking energy and money still hasn't been translated so speed see I'm now back to how fast can I work compressed time is money most people don't even understand the concept like what does that even mean they say it but they don't know what it means yeah oh it's a cute saying it's a perfect t shirt but they're not actually applying it to their life no they're like what does that mean man what does it mean time is money right how do you multiply time how do you buy time rich people buy time so never say I can't afford it I would my rich dad forbid his son and me to say the words I can't he says ask yourself how can I know like the reason I have so much money is because I don't say I can't do it just go how can I do it and just go and do it I make a lot of mistakes but that's how I learn how can I the poorest the poor people like my poor dad always said I can't afford it do you think I made up money I'm school teacher I can't do that and I picked that up and my rich dad never said those words so when I meet poor people they use the words I can't a lot you know it's like my wife Kim is gorgeous you know absolutely drop dead gorgeous the first thing I said she won't go out me you know my friends kept saying she'll never go out with you I said well if I left that stop me she never will so I asked her out for six months so do that I mean it's what goes on between this year and in our hearts that determine our lives out there there's no world out there except what's going on here so the people that say I can't afford it I can't do this I can't get the college the rich are evil you know I choose not to participate that and that's one thing people could change today correct right now is that dialogue in their head stop saying the word can't I can't right so how can I especially as in can't afford it how can I afford that because that opens them up to looking at it as an investment to a greater future right you know when I borrowed 300 million dollars I couldn't do it when until I went to ask and I got turned down so many times I said you know and every time I show the bank of my financials and they go or I aid look do me a favour why did you turn me down and he tell me if this is out your numbers are out there so if I get these numbers fixed can I can see you again he goes sure and he turned me down again but didn't go back and I put id make sure the numbers were real and fix it so it's called rejection you know same as my wife rejected me for six months it's just a matter of personal willpower which is spiritual just saying if that can do it I can do it and how can I think as you once said words flesh yep you think people you think warren buffet reading just to be the majority of you are poor because you real poor stuff you watch poor stuff you on Instagram watching fights . you just scrolling through like you ain't got a life for real some of y'all on Instagram you're on there for 30 minutes if I ask you what you saw you only know you're just scrolling through that's a poverty mindset rich people don't waste time they realize it's their most important commodity they don't watch a lot of TV they don't do a lot of entertainment if they're not working they're studding their craft and getting better at their craft oh you okay I'm sorry okay let me say it one more time there was a language that I needed to learn does it I need to abandon the learn the language that I learned absolutely not does it mean I need to put on a certain type listen to me when I do corporate I promise you I look like this I probably don't look this good sometimes I got on shorts and a t shirt in corporate why because I don't need to necessarily conform they're not asking me to come to dress up but I'm so good at what I do they don't even require a suit are you hearing what I'm saying some of us don't want to wear a suit but you're not on that level though or you want to wear a suit and act as if your suit is going to compensate for what you are inferior at your suit don't make your language sweet read some of you wearing suits because you think like you're going to impress somebody with a suit and you might get in the door but sooner or whoa what are you later I was like I quitting my mom's like don't you dare quit you're to embarrass me you got a wife and kids does YouTube have insurance does YouTube a 401k and I was like you main trying to be funny and rid ain't trying to be disrespectful I love you but you can't teach me how to be a millionaire because you're not one you come from the working class and I'm not mad at you m we wouldn't be where we are without you but you told me that every generation is supposed to get better so I'll take your values but I won't take your ethic because rich people don't work they think the working class will never get rich it wasn't designed oh yeah okay listen to me this country become a wealthy country because they had employees they didn't have to pay that's not like a rocket science so when this country had to start playing people they want to pay lease the three percent that run the world they're not trying let me let me tell you how I know I'm from Detroit we just laid off 15000 workers and the president of gm. she just got 22 million dollars we got 22 million dollars to get one person when we laid off 15000 people and we took their health care that's already paid for no disrespect to nobody and I ain't playing no victim because I'm not victim rich people don't work they think poor people work poor people go clock in make this an hour rich people go I put them to work and I make this much in house see what happens is you're working for you and your family one they got 40 of you working at one time so they giving of 20 and keeping the 80 off 15000 people that's enough to have 22 million dollars so what you have to decide is are you going to keep being the 99 are you ready to be a part of the 1 percent because it doesn't make a difference where you come from high school dropout it doesn't make a difference when you come from get it doesn't make a difference where you come from sleeping in abandoned buildings it doesn't make difference where you come from a 17 year old mom that got pregnant it doesn't make difference when you come from south side of Chicago it doesn't make a difference where you come from pretty much raised in Detroit it doesn't make a difference where you come from took 12 years to get a four year degree it doesn't take a make a difference you know what makes a difference what makes a difference is when become a 99 or a 1and when I start thinking lie acting like ad behaving like a 1% everything changed is that clear.

## LET'S KNOW ABOUT SUCCESS

The first rule of success is to have a vision you see if you don't have a vision of where you go and if you don't have a goal where you daft around and you never end up anywhere I mean as you know I was born in 1947 in Austria after the second world war so I was very fortunate that I stumbled under my vision and I didn't really like Austria when I grew up I couldn't wait to get out of there I couldn't see myself becoming a farmer or a worker in a factory or anything like that even though my parents wanted me to stay there and have a normal life but that was their vision not mine my vision was totally different I felt that I was born for something special for something unique for something big then one day I went to school I remember was 11 years old and they showed documentary about America they showed this documentary the huge skyscrapers the high rises the huge bridges the six lane freeways and all of this stuff in the same reserve that's where I want to be I don't want be around here with these little farm houses and these title buildings I want to be in a America one day after school I walked by a store in Graz so I went inside and I look around and then I saw a magazine it's a body building that had reg park on the cover re gar was then three time minister universe and I saw him on the big screen as Hercules I read that ad I said to myself wow this is the blueprint for my life this is exactly what I want to do I want to become a bodybuilding champion just like rage park i want to get movie just like rich park and i want to make millions of dollars and be rich and famous just like reg park do you know how great felt that I knew where I was going imagine the majority of people don't know where they're going I knew I was going hat I'm going to become this bodybuilding champion just like him so it was just a question of how do you do it I was so relieved because when you have a goal when you have a vision everything becomes easy so people always ask me when they saw me in the gym in the pumping iron days they aid what is it that you're working out so hard five hours a day six hours a day and you have always a smile on your face and I told people all the time I said because to me I shooting for gold in front of me is the Mr. universe title so every rep that I do gets me closer to accomplishing that chord to make this core. This vision turn into reality every single set that I do every repetition every weight that I lift will get me a step closer to turn this goal into reality so I couldn't wait to do another 500 pound squat I couldn't wait to do another 500 pound bench press I couldn't wait to do other 2000 reps of sit ups I couldn't wait for the next exercise with the age of 20 I went to London and I won the Mr. universe contest as the youngest Mr. universe ever ad it was because I had a goal so let me tell you something visualizing your goal and going after it makes it fun you've got to have a purpose no matter what you do In life you've got to have a purpose but you have to do something every day that scares you and mind that's uh a take-off from Helen Keller who said or not said uh she was deaf dumb everything she couldn't do anything and she said every day she did something to scare herself well If you and I had all those afflictions just getting out of bed would be scary enough and I decided that one of the differentiations between the people that got the most out of the week long seminar and the yearlong free mentoring for me is people that really pressed themselves hard so I translated that into they've got to do something and list it what they did to scare themselves every single day that the essence of really what you do is getting people to make more risk or to get out of their comfort zones and then the wealth comes later it's not just of their comfort zones it's the change of reality okay you know your reality is different than my reality and you now your followers realities are all different uh but it's to change your reality and you make yourself uh accountable that's not getting outside your comfort zone making yourself accountable okay uh not just accountable not accountable to somebody else accountable to you me you know yourself because that's the ultimate uh ultimately that's only person you should be accountable to is yourself and we grow up in my judgment wrongly that the that we don't hold ourselves accountable enough we just don't we we've learned to come up with reasons why we can't this reasons why it's okay not to do this reasons why you didn't follow upon time reasons why I told the guy id get back to him by Wednesday it's now Friday oh it's the weekend i'll now get back to him till you know him till you know on Monday and uh life has gotten simpler now with the internet and with email and the things where the communication is almost instant you think it should be easier but it's not I use the analogy 25 30 years ago you're going to buy a 100 million company your due diligence would be there four five weeks and it'd take you there for five weeks to close the deal okay a month and a half six to eight weeks with the internet it should take less time because the information is instantaneous it take us twice as long as close a deal now twice as long there's no reason for that things haven't gotten twice as complicated but somebody has to put their name on the line somebody wants to push off the accountability somebody would rather have brain sign off on it so I go home early on a Thursday knowing you're going to come in early on a Monday and your signature will be on the document instead of mine because I don't want to be accountable and so the kids today have this need it's like thirst for guidance and the kids do better in the yearlong mentor program than the older kids so the kids their teens and twenties uh do better than the guys in their 40s 50s that's because the guys IN their 40's and 50s got a lot of baggage bad habits you know it's tough to get rid them and the um you know motivation gets you started good habits knew you going most people just have piss poor habits and you know I've had these same habits for about 50yeasr now okay about 50 years and I don't even think about I mean it's just like brushing my teeth taking a shower I just do it and uh and I and one of other interviews that uh I did with you I said when I do feel whimpers which isn't too often I just say come on and I just go out and do it uh and I do that about my entire life uh everything about it and I know that if I had to build up these habits 20 30 years ago you know at age 70 I certainly wouldn't be doing this I don't fail very often I do fail you're pretty open about all the failures yeah I'm not ashamed of them rights that's who that's what made me who I am you said failure is just testing correct it's just testing and I don't know and I'm quick to pull the trigger two ways I'm quick to pull the trigger two ways I'm quick trigger and trying something and I'm quick to pull the trigger and closing something just turn the key what does that mean close the business most the people watching this thing should either not be in business if they've got one or close the down if they got one because you got in business for all the wrong reasons and you have the ballots close them down because of what other people are going to say you don't have no idea how limitless it is when you're not afraid of what other people think or say you have no idea there's not two people watching this thing that even has a concept what it is to act as if you have no limits to your abilities zero lack of self-esteem lack of self-worth now they think have self-worth they because they've made a few bucks but in actuality and when they measure it against the other eight ten twelve people sitting around the table they realize or they start to question hell may be I was just lucky now all of us when you're a one trick guy or gal think was I lucky now I've done it so many times I know I m I wasn't lucky I might have been lucky the first time but I haven't been lucky the 15 20 45 I know that okay but maybe I was lucky the first time but my life changed when I went I was pretty much a haphazard kid got a lot of trouble got arrested four or five times thrown in jail and this is with my dad as a cop but then I went I volunteered for the draft un in 1996 at the height of the Vietnam war and uh I went to ocs and that changed my life because it was the really first real high performance thing I could measures myself against other with other people two thirds of all fortune 500 CEOs have one thing in common military background really two thirds of those something else martial arts what do you learn in martial arts brain discipline focus a lot of people don't believe they deserve to be there I convince them and we have these drills why you belong there a lot of people that come there you own with money that have made money think they made it by accident right I just had one of my superstars whose made a hundred million bucks tell me in the last week you know I'm to urge I'm going to have another lucky accident and I said you did it mean you I know you tried a lot of things I believe Thomas Edison I would I wouldn't have done it ten thousand times okay I would hire an engineer from met to do it but mean uh I've tried a lot things nobody failed at more things than I have and the first hundred million are successes but I could write a book about failures that would be I mean because I've tried a lot of different things because failure is just testing and uh one of the reasons I've been so successful generating this equity ad value I my kids and I call all kids is because inconvenience him that making a mistake is okay your parents probably told you can be anything you want but you can't that's horse you can't if it's' all juxtaposed so but what you tell him is that you can anything you want that you have passion for because that eliminates most of the crap because most of the people don't follow their dream you know like they say I the sound of music you can't have a dream come true unless you have a dream now I still dream of Technicolor I say my affirmations and goals every single night it's bloody hard to be a high performance person 74 % hate their job in America now there not much different when you come to Europe the majority of people don't like what they're doing because they're really not doing it because they don't have a goal and they followed the score they just aimlessly drift sound and then all of sudden there's a job opening so they get their job because you have to work but then you work it's a chore it's a work it's not a fun so if you think about a quarter of the people really enjoy what they're doing I life that is unbelievable if you think it so I felt so blessed that I knew what was doing it's like a medical student that studies and knows he wants the become a doctor you know where to go and the same thing is also I politics I remember that in politics I had a very clear vision that I will be the leader of California this is as far as I could go because I was not born in America so I could not run for president so being the governor of the fifth largest state of I should say the largest state the fifth largest economy in the world was for me really the ultimate title the ultimate accomplishment in politics so even though people came up to me says why don't you go and rum for something smaller you're never gonna make it I ran for governor and then two months later become governor of the state of California again because I had a very clear vision what I'm gonna do with California so that's

**Rule #1:** Have vision

**Rule #2 :** Don't listen to the naysayers

Everything I ever did the thing that they heard out of people's mouth was that's impossible that can't be done or no that I exactly what I heard and of course I proved to the people that it can't be done so whenever someone said to me it can't be done I heard it can be done when they said no I heard yes and when they said it's impossible I heard I may be a strong believer what Nelson Mandela said that everything is always impossible until someone does it well I'm gonna be the one that said to myself I'm gonna do it and I'm gonna show it to them maybe it has never been done before that's perfectly in with me but I'm gonna do it and I did not listen to the naysayers.

## 10 HABITS OF ALL SUCCESSFUL PEOPLE

Success means different things to different people for some success might be financial achievements becoming millionaire forex. For some it right means accolades for sportsmen it may mean trophies championships or medals for being successful night simply mean achieving a state of wellness health or happiness whatever it means to you take note of these 10 habits of all successful people they apply to any area and any meaning of success no one they set goals you 'mean probably never met a successful person who doesn't set goals because the chance of you finding what you want without a clear target to move forward are right around zero ids you don't know where you're going you will end up someplace you didn't plan to be setting goals should be the:

**No.1** Priority for anyone seeking success defines exactly what it is you want your end goal to break down exactly what is required to get their many goals to make sure your why your reason for doing what you use do is strong so when you hit those roadblocks when things go wrong as they always do you have the strength and purpose to keep going.

**No.2** They keep responsibility for their life another key attribute of all successful people is they take complete responsibility for the success and the failures in their life unlike the majority they never play the victim role if something doesn't work out they don't blame others they learn the lesson learn one more way not to do something and move on quickly your energy is always best spent in the present and planning for the future your thought process should always be how can I make this work and what can I learn from this never living in the past or making excuses as to why you aren't where you should remember everyone suffers setbacks everyone has the opportunity to either blame others I circumstances or to focus on moving on and creating a better future regardless of what has happened you decide what you do now.

**No.3** They have great self-discipline is a strong trait of all successful people and it can be developed with consistent use anyone that works from home or unsupervised knows the importance of self-discipline when you are alone will you choose to go through social media watch cat videos on YouTube or do something that will be beneficial for you future it is much easier to have discipline if you have clear goals and a meaningful purpose something that is much more important than meaningless distractions.

**No.4** They are obsessed with self-development you can't claim to be successful if you have given up working on yourself this doesn't mean you are never satisfied just that you know it is human nature to want to grow and learn new things be open to learn new things and develop your mind through mentors audiobooks and reading the more you learn the more you will earn financially and spiritually.

**No. 5** They read a lot of reading is a common pastime of many highly successful people the majority these days can't sit alone for two minutes without becoming bored picking up their phone to go on social media probably to post about how bored they are successful people, however, are almost always happy to be alone in quiet to have the opportunity to read or listen to something that will benefit their mind and their future and their future if you're not a reader try audiobooks you can play them in your car in the gym or while you shower and use the time that might normally be wasted to gain new skills new strengths.

**No.6** They manage their time well time management Is essential to success unsuccessful people get stressed and overwhelmed when there are too many tasks on their to-do list successful people are rarely phased they prioritize the big payoff and most rewarding tasks first and leave the insignificant ones o last knowing it matters most to do the most valuable tasks first unsuccessful people plan days weeks months ahead knowing clearly what needs to be done to complete their jobs and reach their goals.

**No.7** They take risks if you don't buy a ticket you can't win the raffle if you don't take big risks you can't achieve big rewards successful people know that there will be times they will need to take risks to get where they need to go often most people won't take those risks for fear of failure however the greater failure to successful people would be that of regret risk going for the life you want or guarantee living with the one you don't want.

**No. 8** They keep going when they suffer failure and setbacks we all suffer setbacks every single person that attempts to live their dream life will suffer through failure many of them might see lose everything must quit the successful never quit they keep going knowing their greatest character is formed in adversity knowing their success story is being written in every moment and it will be especially good now they have a comeback story.

**No.9** They find a way to win successful people find a way period whatever life throws their way they deal with it dodge it smash through it whatever is required they find a way to win it's the whatever it takes mentality it's the confidence in knowing whatever happens I will give my all and leave nothing on the table I will find a way to win.

**No.10** They do what they love if you're not doing what you love you can't claim yourself a success spending the majority of your hours also known as the majority of your life doing the thing you hate for money is not successful living its torture to the soul if you need to suffer doing something you don't like to get to a life you love do that but do to lose sight of exactly that your ultimate purpose find your life purpose think of all the things you love to do more than anything in the world then brainstorm how you can turn those passion into profit doing what you love every day even if you are taking a pay cut it will be worth it do what you love every day and you will never work a day in your life.

You have the power to create meaning in your life rather than passively look for it.

MAKE THIS MOMENT THE MOMENT OF TRUTH ABOUT YOURSELF YOU ARE LEAVING A LEGACY WHETHER YOU WANT TO OR NOT EVERYBODY IN THIS ROOM IS GOING TO LEAVE A LEGACY. THE QUESTION IS, ARE YOU GOING TO BE INTENTIONAL. About the legacy, you're leaving? I do not care what other people think of me for having goals and dreams for myself. For some reason, everybody doesn't want to follow through. Everybody talks about a good game, but I need you to follow through. And no disrespect but this is why I need you to get your motives to be pure. And some of you, you have big dreams, but your energy is like a triple battery. Your battery has to be able to push those dreams. And if you've got a small engine, you're not going to be able to push it. If you want to be an anomaly, you have to act like one. Like people want all these special things to happen but then they're acting like everybody else. So, for me, I create the meaning. And meaning to me is, do I know more about the world today than I did yesterday? That enhances meaning for me. There is a direct connection between finding your passion and reaching your potential. You can't give anyone ownership of what is going to happen to you. A question opens the mind, a statement closes the mind. So, when you say I can't afford it your mind shuts down and you become what you say. My lack of interest in complaining is so high and when I watch what people complain about it breaks my heart because they completely lack perspective. We gain a greater perspective when we zoom out. And too many of you are guilty of becoming what you are going through. You are not what you are going through now is your time. Now is the moment to capture the vision.

I challenge you today, don't wait to be second or third going to be the first.

Here it is, you're trying to accomplish something. Here it is you're trying to do something and yet there's some fear right because you've never seen anybody do it before. You're not sure if you're going to make it. Go ahead and accept the pressure of being the first. You'll be faced with difficult situations. There'll be times that you don't believe in your ability to persevere. There'll be times you feel incapable of rising to meet the challenges that face you.

You'll be tempted to turn your back and run. But running is never the best option. When you're in the middle of a struggle the only way out is through. People with vision can see what other people can't see. You're going to a storm, right, are you hearing me? You're on your way to a storm, you're actually in a storm or you're coming out. It's part of life, so I don't care if you're a star athlete, I don't care if you're a billionaire, I don't care if you're a CEO,

I don't care who you are. You can go to the moon, we all have problems. What I'm trying to tell you is this though, don't be consumed with them. Problems are a part of life but guess what, they're not life. I want you to focus on your dreams. Rather than running away from obstacles or trying to figure out some kind of way around them, go right through them. Brace yourself, steady your nerves, put your head down. I need you to build. This is your building years, this is not your bitter years. These are your building years, you're building a legacy. You're building something for your children. You're building something for your children's children. You're building something for your wife that's on the way. You're building something for your husband that's on the way. You're building something not just for your first name but your last name. You're building something that's why God put you on the earth. He didn't put you on the earth just to exist. He put you on the earth to build something. He put you on the earth to break something. He put you on the earth to demolish something. He put you on the earth to make sure that you produce something and something that would last. The fears you face along the way, they'll make you better. Our biggest fears always carry with them the greatest opportunity for personal growth. Our fears and how we face them bring out the best in us. If something doesn't scare us, if something doesn't challenge us, it doesn't change us.

I need you to see what the next 10 years look like. I need you to see what the next 5 years look like. I need you to see yourself winning. I know that is difficult right now but your vision said you're going to win. I know there's a storm that's coming and raging and whirring against you but you've got to have a vision that keeps you in the fight even when it feels like you're about to quit. The storm may jar you a bit but I promise that you won't buckle and you won't break. If as long as you get peace on the inside all hell can be breaking loose on the outside. And you can speak out what you hold in. The worst storm in the world is not the one on the outside, but when it gets on the inside you can't speak what you do not have. Dare to face your fears dare to take risks dare to be better I'm giving you 4 rules that if you can obey if you can make these rules a command then I believe not only will the pain subside but perhaps transformation could take place from the inside

**Rule #1** - There are no more zero days.

What is a zero-day? A zero-day is when you don't do a single solitary thing towards whatever your dream or goal is in this life I want you to make a conscious decision that there will be more zero days I'm not saying you got to "kill" yourself but the point I'm trying to make is that you need to promise yourself that your new program your new system will be a life lived of no more zero days this means that when the day is over and you look up and it's 11:58 pm you did something no more zero days I don't care if it was one push up, one sit-up, one page of the book you feel me? But just decide that there will be no more zero days. You see, when you're in the vortex of being bummed and you are trapped in the pattern of self-sabotaging behaviour you get used to it and the only way you are going to break out is with a massive string of constant non-zero-days that's rule number one.

**Rule #2-** Be grateful to the 3 yours.

Call it mumbo jumbo if you want to. New flash, the tree yours are the past, you, the present you, and the future you. And if you want to love somebody and have someone to love you back, you have to learn to love yourself and the three yours are key. You have to be grateful for the past you for the positive things you've done and do favours for the future like you would for your best friend. Are you feeling bad today? Stop for a second. And think of a good decision you made yesterday: that salad, that fish, that protein shake instead of the burger or fries. Did you save money in your past? Buy something that resonated with you and thanked you in the past? Are you currently saving toward that dream or that goal you have, or that improbable feat, then you need to be grateful for the present you. The last part of the three yours is you got to love your future self. You got to do your future self a favour. I know you might be tired. You might be addicted to a video game or a television series. Not today's present self, this one's for future me. No PlayStation. No Xbox, no distraction. I don't care if it's one more push-up or one more sit-up or one more page in the book. You see the cycle of doing something for someone else, future you, and thanking someone for the good in your life, past you is the key to building gratitude and productivity. Don't doubt me. Over time, you should spread that gratitude to others who have helped you on your path.

**Rule #3** - Forgive yourself

I mean it. Maybe you have all the know-how, the money, the ability, strength, and talent to do whatever you want to do, but let's say you still don't do it. Now you're going to give yourself a tough time for not doing what you need to do. Pick your head up. Being disappointed in yourself causes you to be less productive. If you can forgive yourself, you can be healed from the past, equipped for the present, and cast vision for the future. You owe you, forgive you, and get on with the rest of your life.

**Rule #4** - Exercise and books

Is the easiest and it's three words. Exercise and books. That's it, pretty standard advice. But when you exercise daily, you get smarter. You get crystal clear about the road ahead. When you exercise you position yourself to win the war. When you exercise and you push yourself, you test the limitations of your soul and you will become crystal clear both internally and externally. That all you have is all you need. As for books, almost everything we've ever thought or felt or gone through or wanted or wanted to know how to do has been figured out by someone else. So get some books. Read seven habits of highly successful people. Read emotional intelligence. Read from good to great. Rethinking fast and slow read books that will help you understand read books that will get you crystal clear on your future. Read the bodyweight, fitness, Reddit, and incorporate it into your workouts. Reading gets you to the next level faster. One last piece of advice though, if you wake up tomorrow and you can't remember the four rules, I just laid it out for you.

This is how you can dominate and get an unfair, competitive advantage in the marketplace and the game of life. And this is the road to self-improvement physically, emotionally, mentally, you got this man. Some of you are holding on to some really good memories that are no longer current memories, and you need to let them go so that you can get what's next.

So we're gonna do we're gonna get the right information and then we're gonna get narrow-focused and boom were gonna go for it are you hearing what I'm saying that's it many of you will not be successful because you've got this giant goal and no steps to go with it. You're just in your mind like "girl this is my year!" how many steps? I don't know. Like what is it going to take for me to do it? I don't know. I just know this is my year. Can I be real with you?

If you can't measure it, it ain't real.

Keep your dreams phenomenal. Keep your vision phenomenal. Keep it phenomenal, and now I need you to get your weight up. As an individual, I need you to get your schedule up. I need you to get your life up. I need you to get your words up. I need you to get your heart up. I need you to get your act up.

I need you to get to a place where every single thing that you do is phenomenal so that the life you want to live you can live that life. And say I ain't going nowhere. I will break you. You will not defeat me! You will not destroy me! Some of you are so ignorant. You've been through so much hell. You're gonna quit now!? Why me, God? Why did I get ms? Why did I get cancer? Why did my momma die? Why did I get fired? Do you understand? Listen! You got through that. You got put through that because what that does, that tension, produces greatness! Stop running from it and run to it! Stop telling me what you're going through. The Greats they get to, they go through it and the harder it is the better we're gonna put in work. Because every time you put in work, you get the same consequences you get paid. You get rewarded. And when you're out there dealing with the real world, it ain't pretty. You've got to have a heart. Get some hearts. The only time you get right now is to believe. Your job is simple, all you've got to do is believe. Believe it could happen anyway. But most importantly, believe it could happen for you. I know you believe it could happen but you have trouble believing it could happen for you. Believe the time is now. You've got one job: to believe and convince you. Just believe because once you believe. It's easy to block out the noise. It's easy to block out the haters. It's easy to block out ignorance. It's easy to block out the liars. It's easy to block out the lies inside your mind. You were made for a time such as this. You were made to achieve today. You were made to make the impossible possible. I mean the Wright brothers are human.

Thomas Edison, human. Michael Jordan. Oprah. She's human.

I am talking to you right now, listen to me, you are human which means it is possible but you've got to go do it how. No more time to waste. No more time to fret. You gotta do it now. You gotta do it bravely. You gotta do it, scared. You gotta do it gently. You gotta do a lot, don't care, just do it. Whatever you must do, go and do it because the impossible is possible today. The world is waiting to talk about you. The world is waiting to brag about you. The world is waiting to follow you on social media. The world is ready for you to be an influencer. The world is ready to hear your voice. The world is waiting on you. Success is waiting for you. Winning is waiting for you. Achievement is waiting for you. Because you are a winner. You are focused. You are determined. You are a fighter. Say it to me.

I win. I achieved it. It is possible. I win. I achieved it. It is possible.

No turning back. No quitting this time. No hesitation. No procrastination. The impossible is now possible because you've got your mind made up, you got your mind focused in life, you have to sometimes do the impossible to get what is possible. In life, you have to stand up for what you believe in. In life, you have to work so hard to achieve what is possible. Cause here's why: ain't nobody giving it away. Nobody's going to do it for you. You've got to take this journey, and you've got to take it for yourself, and you've got to take it by yourself. So listen to me, don't let yourself off the hook. That setback, you've got an excuse but don't take it. That justification, you've got an excuse but don't use it. You've got you "out," but you can't use you "out." Because if you use your out, you ain't gonna do the impossible. Possible is going to become your reality. What is impossible is possible. The easiest thing I've done was to get out from under the labels and to live the life that I live. The most difficult thing I have done was to believe that I can do it. It the moment you realize everything In your life has come to a point where you can either stay where you are or you can pick up your bags build the courage to move that inch to move that inch in order to build even just the slightest bit of momentum life is a series of fight I mean think about it you're either in a fight just got out of a fight but trust me there's a fight right around the corner just waiting for your life is going to beat upon you in so many ways and many things they come back you know negative thoughts and how you feel about yourself they don't die they come back once you stop doing the maintenance work on your mind one inch is all it takes it's the time in your life where it's do or die what are you gonna do it's the time when you're feeling like you're scraping the bottom of the barrel you're in the dark but it's up to you to change your perception to shed some light on where you are listening to motivational messages going to seminars and workshops spending time quietly listening to the still small voice within who am I really is this really me am giving my best a I just reflecting what's around me because all of these various things affect how we show up in life when think about fighting I'm not talking about people I'm talking about situations I'm talking about circumstances I'm talking about opportunities that something you have to fight for right now whenever you are as you are today you have enough right now to build the legacy that you really want it's a time when you're ready to give up but you know if you do you'll never be able to live with yourself with the guilt and shame of not pulling yourself out of this state which way are you going to turn things may happen to you and things will happen around you but the most important things the things that happen in you and you have to stand up inside yourself and deal with it and handle it now is the time to start building your legacy now is the moment to start making their impact you got to get into position baby so I know life is hard sometimes I know life can be up and down but right now I need you to get in position to fight what's your position to fight what's your mindset to fight what's your mentality when you about to fight you get ready to fight you know a fight's coming your adrenaline begins to pump your heart begins to race your mind gets right and say look I'm not gonna just fight I'm gonna win this battle and suck are you going down and I'm not talking about people I'm talking about circumstances I'm talking about situations and I'm talking about opportunities so here's the first thing we got to figure out first you have to acknowledge who you fight and I'm not talking about people I'm talking about you the number one person you gonna fight is yourself so are you fighting procrastination are you fighting excuses are you fighting low self-esteem ladies and gentlemen get your dukes up get your hands up and get ready to fight see let me tell you something trouble can be a bully but you better learn how to land the first blow lesson number one acknowledge the fight who are you fighting who is your battle with key number two what is your strategy to win are you going for the knockout blow are you gonna kill him softly with a couple of jabs you might be in a situation right now where the doctor said to you that you're not healthy your body's family you might even have cancer oh that's not just a battle that's going to be a war ladies and gentlemen but to win fights you got to punch and counter punch jab and jab back let me tell you something life is a series of fights the worst thing you can do is run away from your fights because if life is a series of fights and you run away you just ran away from your life your promotion is in the fight your promotion and your next level is about you get into this war get into this battle with winning here's the reality i don't believe in getting bullied i believe in altercations and so let me tell you something it's trouble coming your way a fight's coming your way you running from your fight you just ran from your life and you just ran from your future I've been fighting my whole life and let me tell you something we're gonna battle baby and I want you to do the same thing because when you get victory you'll raise your arms up like the champ when you come over depression you raise your arms like a champ when you overcome bankruptcy you raise your arms like a champ will you come up with divorce raise your arms and victory I love Muhammad Ali because he did it with charisma I float like a butterfly sting like a bee rumble man rumble let me tell you something you got to be ready to fight because your life is all about fights here's reality life can be messy but you gotta clean it up and you better learn how to fight well here it is a wake-up call a reality check a time to realize that it just got real and there's nothing at this point in time right now you can do about it except figure out a way how to get through it yeah many people right now are angry and complaining and scared and don't know what to do yes there's something happening right now in our world in our society and many people right now just don't know what to do but remember there was a time you went about your day without a care in the world you just did what you had to do you moved the way you wanted to move you did what you wanted to do but now things have changed things just got real but you have to ask yourself what's next what am i going to just complain or am I going i got to learn to adapt and overcome like animals in the world birds lions tigers all different species of life that are not human but yet they understand the significance of what it means to survive regardless of what they're going through they still figure out how to survive how to live how to move how to push but you as a human being you'll just sit around and complain and worry not knowing exactly what it is to do next living is all you can do keeping faith being strong overcoming adversity and realizing that yeah not going to always be a good day but it's definitely a great day it's a great day for me to learn about what I am capable of what am I willing to do how am I gonna push forward instead of pushing back what's my next decision what's my next path what direction am I going because what's surrounding me doesn't necessarily mean that it's breaking me to a point where I can't function you have to have the ability to understand that if you don't build up something it'll never have true foundation it will never have balance it will never understand purpose there won't be any purpose to it because you're too busy being what you think you ought to be instead of knowing what you need to be this is a reality check this is the time to find out what you can do how you can get above it how you could go beyond it how you can look up to the sky instead of looking down at the dirt this is that opportunity ladies and gentlemen don't be afraid now be strong don't be weak be powerful don't worry about the things you cannot control make the most of what you have and from the bottom of my heart conduct your business start your day off with a grateful heart and let that be the spark of light that pulls you from the dark mark Bryan said gratitude is the most powerful emotion you will ever feel and thank you are the most powerful words you will ever say see when you display a grateful spirit the universe will hear it the heavens above will cheer it and the demons below will fear it so please let's all practice gratitude on a daily basis and never forget to say thank you for the life the good lord gave us it may not be rainbows and sunshine all the time but i guarantee if you take a moment to reflect you will definitely find a reason to be thankful for your heart and a reason to show gratitude for your mind or better yet what about that time when you almost did you know what but out of nowhere you got a sign and you got out of that situation just in the nick of time so that means you should say thank you for your intuition and you yes you should say thank you to the person that paid your tuition because you prayed for it and it came to fruition and you should say thank you for your two good ears because you have the ability to listen and you heard those snakes hissing and you knew it was time to abort that mission say thank you for your heart that knows how to mend when it's broken show gratitude for your composure that helps you control your emotions say thank you for your inner strength that help you overcome drinking and smoking show gratitude for your will that never allows whining and moping say thank you for your optimism that keeps you wishing and hoping show gratitude for your sense of humour that keeps you laughing smiling and joking the same sense of humour that helped you put the pieces back together when you were broken show gratitude my friend because you're a child it's golden William ward once said feeling gratitude and not expressing it it's like wrapping a present and not giving it i say what good is it to feel the joy of gratitude in your heart and not be showing it and not be Living it say thank you for what you do have no matter how great or no matter how small because there are many others who are not so blessed but they have absolutely nothing at all say thank you for your failure setbacks and pitfalls because they help you revise your plan and pointed out a lot of your flaws which is the exact reason for your present-day success so please be grateful for the obedience you had to not be stubborn and figure out the message in your mess if you're able to walk be thankful because many are not so blessed if you were able to study retain and pass with an a be grateful because many others failed the exact same test say thank you for the courage you had to remove all your toxic friends show gratitude for all of your losses that eventually led to all of your wins say thank you for the love and affection you're able to give be grateful for the gift of life and the ability to give it your all because you only have one life to live say thank you for your sense of smell because mama's cooking always smells so good show gratitude for the determination you had to overcome and make it out to hood because many were not so blessed say thank you for your worst days because they help you truly appreciate when you're at your best say thank you thank you thank you be grateful for your talent because all the scouts rank your number one so please never take that for granted and show gratitude for your parents that gave you great wisdom and planted seeds that you were able to water and watch blossom and exceed even your wildest expectations gratitude is the key this is a fact not a rumour so show gratitude and be thankful today for the success you already have coming to you in the future this is a great day to win you.

Small and steady wins the race what's the debauched way to variation your life I contemplate it's comprehended how to arrange daily routine with discontinuous brain and body training and killing procrastination. The little win, with your family and you, feel like watching the TV set you up for another when a little wind sets you up for another win the next day, a little win of getting up at 5 o'clock and running your morning routine sets you up for a habit, of a 5 am morning routine 5 a.m. morning with him small daily improvements over time will lead you to stunning results. Or comes down to this Elvis, I think you have to work hard like just so everybody knows we haven't got against this subject yet occupied hard, is the course of entry to anything you know zero successful people that don't work their face of you know zero people now they may have money as mom and dad made money and have it too them but people that build their success you know zero people that have had the success that did not put in an obnoxious amount of work.

What's the most important key to success? I think it's hunger. It's not getting satisfied, a hungry that doesn't go, a hungry to leaders, a hunger to grow, a hunger to serve, a hunger to give, a hungry to create breakthroughs most people W hungry until they make a certain amount of money and then they get comfortable and there nothing wrong with that but it's not about the money is not about the business is about your growth because every one of us either grows or does. People ask me all the time what it takes to be happy? I say one word: progress. Progress equals happiness because achieving a goal feels good for how long? A week a month, three months? And then they need to be something else and the reason for something else is because you gotta grow to envisage a discussion with your future self and then let's imagine that you of twenty years from now shows up at your doorstep and that you are stronger, smarter, wiser, wealthier, healthier, happier and that you showed up at your door and looks at your life and looks you in the eye of that future you are going to give you advice on what to stop, what to start. What's the first thing they would tell you to be? Or do I? Take a step back right now and think about who we all admire in the world right? They are all people that pointed to the system, they are people that practice singing since they were five, there are people that shoot 10000 baskets every morning. It's always that 99 percent of people right now that are listening to this are playing in the middle, they are playing the game that was structured for them, the risk-averse, they are great, and most importantly, they fear what other people think. Look I believe that with lots of goodness in us but life throws curveballs, life, the ambition of being alive, helps us dream, and if you have been given a dream don't discount that because you are not good enough yet develop yourself, weaponize yourself teach yourself to be so good at something necessary to serve in the area of your dream that now you never even think about your comfort zones. Your comfort zone is irrelevant. What matters is what you are trying to do with your life? How are you trying to contribute? The one thing that discipline does help you with, is it helps you get things done and when you get things done, when you do things, you have more success if you have more success, and something big part of success is not being lazy just doing it. It's like 90 percent of it showing up, getting there, and started working like you are not gonna feel perfect every day. It's pretty much the same with everybody that gets good at something. There's gotta be those days you push through, and they are probably gonna be more numerous than the day you don't and so the benefit of discipline in my eyes has always been that through discipline I get things done. Those days when I am tired or worn out or just basically sick of the grind. What do I do on those days? I go anyway. I get it. I get It done even if I'm just going through the motions. I go through the motions. So, you're in school, yes you perhaps are getting grades, etc but if it's not meaningful to you, if it's not important to you then you're not going to make it a priority. So, what you have to do is find out how you can make it meaningful? How can you make it purposeful? How can you make it stick and when you can find that out, I promise you will get up early, you'll get there first and you'll do whatever it takes to make that goal a reality. So, for me, no such thing as procrastination, it's such a thing as it's not a priority to you. This is kind of hard to understand but sometimes you can try so hard at something. Sometimes you can be so prepared and still fail and every time you fail it's painful causes sadness and especially as I saw last night it causes disappointment I've often said man's character is not judged after he celebrates a victory but by what he does when his back is against the wall so no matter how great the setback How severe the failure you never give up, you pick yourself up, you brush yourself off, you push forward, you move on, you adapt, you overcome, that is what I believe everybody here, everybody watching, I won't be stopped, I can't be stopped you're either committed, or you aren't. You're either willing to do everything it takes, whatever that might be or you aren't. You either are willing to go through hell and high water and fire and brimstone to get to your goals or you aren't. Work on yourself, work on your focus you cannot stop, you gotta work the problem with you if you see the difficulty, as something negative I want you to see difficult differently, are you hearing me? I need you to push through that stuff. You can get through it the more you go through, the more difficult it is, the more challenging it is to listen to me, the harder it is. Are you hearing me? The more challenging it is, all you're doing baby is building muscle in life, you're either going through a storm in a storm, or you're coming out. It is a part of life. There's no way around it so just be careful not to allow the trials and tribulations to consume you. I don't care if you're a billionaire. I don't care if you're CEO of one of the most important companies, I don't care if you're an entertainer, like I don't care who you are, you can go to the moon. We all have problems. What I'm trying to tell you is that politics is a part of life but guess what they're not life. It's not going to be easy. There are moments when you are going to doubt yourself. There are rough times that are gonna come but they have not come to stay no matter how bad it is or how bad it gets. You've gotta make it your business to make it happen. For me, it has been the- to be that guy that does what people say can't be done. You know and I think it started with trying to please my mother and trying to please my grandmother and they always wanted higher for me. They always wanted more for me, and it got to the point that I wanted to be something. I wanted to be somebody, and it made me choose certain roles, it made me turn down certain roles. There is more than an image that I want to project. I want to be the person that is the first person there and the last person to leave.

That's what I want to be because I think that the road to success is through commitment and through the strength to drive through that commitment when it gets hard, and it is going to get hard and you're going to want to quit sometimes but it'll be coloured by who you are and more who you want to be. I found that wanting to be an actor stems from wanting to be somebody. My mom wanted me to be a truck driver because that would mean I would make $24000 a year if I went to truck masters and I'll be twice what my father made, and she thought that would happen but something inside of me said I don't want to drive a truck. There's something else that matters more to me, and I decided I was not going to go for the money instead of passion and the reward was pretty amazingly better than being a truck driver. It's not bad being a truck driver, it's just not what I was after and I look back and one of the things that helped me was my original teacher Jim Rohn, who was a personal development speaker I went to hear when. I was 17 he said so the first time I heard him he said you know it's really simple if you want life to change, you got to change. If you want life to be better you've got to get better. It's the only way it happens, and luck will show up for people and it will leave them but if you're constantly improving who you are and what you give, game over. See if you can find some ways to multiply your value to the market and he said your income will immediately start to change. See if you go through life holding back and most of us do, most of us if we have done All we can do? Most of us will have to answer, no we haven't. We've been holding back. We have ideas that we don't act on things we want to do, we're afraid to take chances, we go through life trying to seek security and not coming outside of our comfort zone and we take most of our stuff with us to the grave. Up until then, I was hoping that the economy would change, I was hoping that my company would change, I was hoping that my paycheck would change, I was hoping that circumstances outside would change, and here's what I found out. It isn't going to change.

So, then my question was if it isn't going to change, how will my life ever change, and here's what my teacher taught me. When you change, everything will change for you and I'm saying that the fact that you're still here, that you're still breathing, you've got some more work and you owe it to yourself. You owe it to yourself so when you get up in the morning that you can look yourself in the face and say hey, I'm living my life on my terms. Change your question, change your life.

When it comes to planning your life, I want to get you to learn to ask three questions now. The question you want to ask yourself is what do I want? What's my outcome? What's my result? The word R.P.M. The first one is to get you focused on the target. The target is not the activity, the activity can change. It's what the - what's the result I'm after. If you know exactly what it is you want, what you desire, what you're after, clarity is power. The more clear you are in specifically what you want the faster your brain can get you there but if you're generally saying things like what do I want, ' well you know I want more money, ' fine, here's a dollar get out of here.' Whether you get the outcome or not, whether you get that result will be based firstly on clarity and the second thing is whether you get enough emotional juice to keep going after it when things don't work out. Did you achieve the outcome? Yeah, when you're that general, you might be- you think you're not getting your goal, you are. The way your language your goal, the way you think about it, you're receiving it. You know, I, you know I want to feel a bit better. I want to lose some weight fine; you lost the pound you're done. When you get better, everything will get better for you and that's where I picked up that phrase: for things to change, you've got to change. You don't have to change the marketplace you don't have to change the marketing plan, you don't have to change the economy, you don't have to change countries, you don't have to change circumstances out there, all you've got to do is look within and see if you can change yourself for the better and as you change, things will start to change for you. What's the result I'm after, what is the ultimate result, what do I want out of this week, out of this thing, out of my business, out of my life, for my body. Don't concern yourself too much with how you're going to achieve your goal, leave that completely to a power greater than yourself. All you have to do is know where you're going the answers will come to you of their own accord. Here's my best advice: welcome all experiences, you never know which one is going to turn everything on. Are there going to be some moments when you want to give up? Yes, will there be some moments when it's going to seem like it's impossible, the pain that you're experiencing, the disappointment that you're experiencing that you're going to say it's not worth it? Yes, that's- that's going to be right there for you. It's going to be in your face telling you to go back. When we think about changing our lives usually that means changing your behaviour or retraining yourself, getting new habits, going out and trying them out, and changing your life. This is about changing your thoughts and then your life will change. Change your thoughts Change your life. Benjamin Disraeli said nothing can resist a human that will stake its existence on its purpose. Shortly out, I'll do it or die. Know that all you have to do is hold your goal before you. Everything else will take care of itself and I can tell you that it doesn't make any difference what age you are, whether your teenager watching this or whether you're someone in your 60s, 70s, 80s, or anywhere along the way, you can make that change. Every thought, every feeling, every emotion you experience in this lifetime is shaped by beliefs and values. All of your life is controlled by the decisions you make. Decisions about what to believe, decisions about what to feel, decisions about what to do and most of us are on automatic pilot letting the world trigger us instead of taking back control of our life and when you do that, just think of it this way. Anything you want to change, you want to change your body, you want to change your career, your business, your relationship, what to do requires the right strategy. If you want to lose weight and keep it off you can't just throw your pendulum and go on some silly diet. You have to know the things that are going to give you lasting results, so we teach those strategies, but some people even know what to do but they don't do it and why are we able to get people to do it, to follow through because 80% of success in anything my friends, is psychology and 20% is mechanics. What that means is there's how to do stuff and there's why to do stuff. How to do it is not that complex and if you learn from somebody who knows those refined distinctions they can- they can show you those tipping points. Those things you can do wherein the least amount of time, you get the biggest result. As you look at yourself as a business operator, as you look at yourself as an entrepreneur, as you look at yourself as a person that wants to make a mark with your life, that wants to leave a legacy, you've got to be hungry. It's better to be prepared for an opportunity and not have one than to have an opportunity and not be prepared. You want to find people who master that because success leaves clues and that's the same thing I'm suggesting to you. Whatever area that you want to go in if it's finances and business, the insurance industry, whatever area that you're interested in, find the people who are mastering that and follow their example. Watch your relationship. They are a nourishing relationship and there is a toxic relationship. Nourishing relationships, bring the best out of you, inspire your toxic relationship, they drain you. Hungry people are willing to do the things that others won't do, to have the things tomorrow others won't have. People always strive to get on top in life because it's the bottom that is overcrowded. Hungry people know if you want to be successful, you must be willing to do the things today others won't do, to have the things tomorrow others won't have. If you do what is easy, your life will be hard. Complain, point at your circumstances, give up your power, blame the government, blame the economy. If you do what is easy, your life will be hard but if you do what is hard, your life will be easy. It's hard to make a radical change in your behaviour. It's hard to take ownership, it's hard to swallow the bitter pill that wherever you find yourself, at some point in time you made an appointment to be there. It's hard. It's hard. If you do what is easy, your life will be hard. If you do what is hard, your life will be easy.

# INKFEATHERS PUBLISHING

*India's Most Author Friendly Publishing House*

Stay updated about the latest books, anthologies, events, exclusive offers, contests, product giveaways and other things that we do to support authors.

 Inkfeathers Publishing

 @InkfeathersPublishing

 @_Inkfeathers

 @Inkfeathers

 Inkfeathers.com

*We'd love to connect with you!*

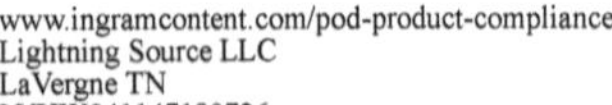